D1608752

BLACK AMERICANS OF ACHIEVEMENT

JAMES FARMER

—— •(•)• ——

Jeff Sklansky

Senior Consulting Editor
Nathan Irvin Huggins
Director
W.E.B. Du Bois Institute for Afro-American Research
Harvard University

CHELSEA HOUSE PUBLISHERS
New York   Philadelphia

Chelsea House Publishers
Editor-in-Chief Remmel Nunn
Managing Editor Karyn Gullen Browne
Copy Chief Mark Rifkin
Picture Editor Adrian G. Allen
Art Director Maria Epes
Assistant Art Director Noreen Romano
Manufacturing Manager Gerald Levine
Systems Manager Lindsey Ottman
Production Manager Joseph Romano
Production Coordinator Marie Claire Cebrián

Black Americans of Achievement
Senior Editor Richard Rennert

Staff for JAMES FARMER
Text Editor Marian W. Taylor
Editorial Assistant Michele Haddad
Picture Researcher Melanie Sanford
Designer Diana Blume
Cover Illustration Robert Caputo

First Printing

1 3 5 7 9 8 6 4 2

Library of Congress Cataloging-in-Publication Data
Sklansky, Jeff.
  James Farmer, civil rights leader/by Jeff Sklansky.
    p. cm.—(Black Americans of achievement)
  Includes bibliographical references and index.
  Summary: Examines the life and career of the black activist.
  ISBN 0-7910-1126-7
      0-7910-1151-8 (pbk.)
  1. Farmer, James, 1920– —Juvenile literature. 2. Afro-
Americans—Biography—Juvenile literature. 3. Civil rights
workers—United States—Biography—Juvenile literature. 4. Afro-
Americans—Civil rights—Juvenile literature. 5. Civil rights
movements—United States—History—20th century—Juvenile lit-
erature. [1. Farmer, James, 1920– . 2. Civil rights workers. 3.
Afro-Americans—Biography.] I. Title. II. Series.
E185.97.F37S55 1991
323.'092—dc20
  [B]
                                    LC 91-8437
                                    CIP
                                    AC

*Frontispiece: James Farmer,
director of the Congress of Racial
Equality (CORE), leads a line of
pickets during a 1964 civil rights
demonstration in San Francisco,
California.*

CONTENTS

BLACK AMERICANS OF ACHIEVEMENT

RALPH ABERNATHY
civil rights leader

MUHAMMAD ALI
heavyweight champion

RICHARD ALLEN
religious leader and social activist

LOUIS ARMSTRONG
musician

ARTHUR ASHE
tennis great

JOSEPHINE BAKER
entertainer

JAMES BALDWIN
author

BENJAMIN BANNEKER
scientist and mathematician

AMIRI BARAKA
poet and playwright

COUNT BASIE
bandleader and composer

ROMARE BEARDEN
artist

JAMES BECKWOURTH
frontiersman

MARY MCLEOD BETHUNE
educator

BLANCHE BRUCE
politician

RALPH BUNCHE
diplomat

GEORGE WASHINGTON CARVER
botanist

CHARLES CHESNUTT
author

BILL COSBY
entertainer

PAUL CUFFE
merchant and abolitionist

FATHER DIVINE
religious leader

FREDERICK DOUGLASS
abolitionist editor

CHARLES DREW
physician

W.E.B. DU BOIS
scholar and activist

PAUL LAURENCE DUNBAR
poet

KATHERINE DUNHAM
dancer and choreographer

MARIAN WRIGHT EDELMAN
civil rights leader and lawyer

DUKE ELLINGTON
bandleader and composer

RALPH ELLISON
author

JULIUS ERVING
basketball great

JAMES FARMER
civil rights leader

ELLA FITZGERALD
singer

MARCUS GARVEY
black-nationalist leader

DIZZY GILLESPIE
musician

PRINCE HALL
social reformer

W. C. HANDY
father of the blues

WILLIAM HASTIE
educator and politician

MATTHEW HENSON
explorer

CHESTER HIMES
author

BILLIE HOLIDAY
singer

JOHN HOPE
educator

LENA HORNE
entertainer

LANGSTON HUGHES
poet

ZORA NEALE HURSTON
author

JESSE JACKSON
civil rights leader and politician

JACK JOHNSON
heavyweight champion

JAMES WELDON JOHNSON
author

SCOTT JOPLIN
composer

BARBARA JORDAN
politician

MARTIN LUTHER KING, JR.
civil rights leader

ALAIN LOCKE
scholar and educator

JOE LOUIS
heavyweight champion

RONALD MCNAIR
astronaut

MALCOLM X
militant black leader

THURGOOD MARSHALL
Supreme Court justice

ELIJAH MUHAMMAD
religious leader

JESSE OWENS
champion athlete

CHARLIE PARKER
musician

GORDON PARKS
photographer

SIDNEY POITIER
actor

ADAM CLAYTON POWELL, JR.
political leader

LEONTYNE PRICE
opera singer

A. PHILIP RANDOLPH
labor leader

PAUL ROBESON
singer and actor

JACKIE ROBINSON
baseball great

BILL RUSSELL
basketball great

JOHN RUSSWURM
publisher

SOJOURNER TRUTH
antislavery activist

HARRIET TUBMAN
antislavery activist

NAT TURNER
slave revolt leader

DENMARK VESEY
slave revolt leader

MADAM C. J. WALKER
entrepreneur

BOOKER T. WASHINGTON
educator

HAROLD WASHINGTON
politician

WALTER WHITE
civil rights leader and author

RICHARD WRIGHT
author

ON
ACHIEVEMENT
———— ❧ ————

Coretta Scott King

BEFORE YOU BEGIN this book, I hope you will ask yourself what the word excellence means to you. I think that it's a question we should all ask, and keep asking as we grow older and change. Because the truest answer to it should never change. When you think of excellence, perhaps you think of success at work; or of becoming wealthy; or meeting the right person, getting married, and having a good family life.

Those important goals are worth striving for, but there is a better way to look at excellence. As Martin Luther King, Jr., said in one of his last sermons, "I want you to be first in love. I want you to be first in moral excellence. I want you to be first in generosity. If you want to be important, wonderful. If you want to be great, wonderful. But recognize that he who is greatest among you shall be your servant."

My husband, Martin Luther King, Jr., knew that the true meaning of achievement is service. When I met him, in 1952, he was already ordained as a Baptist preacher and was working towards a doctoral degree at Boston University. I was studying at the New England Conservatory and dreamed of accomplishments in music. We married a year later, and after I graduated the following year we moved to Montgomery, Alabama. We didn't know it then, but our notions of achievement were about to undergo a dramatic change.

You may have read or heard about what happened next. What began with the boycott of a local bus line grew into a national movement, and by the time he was assassinated in 1968 my husband had fashioned a black movement powerful enough to shatter forever the practice of racial segregation. What you may not have read about is where he got his method for resisting injustice without compromising his religious beliefs.

He adopted the strategy of nonviolence from a man of a different race, who lived in a distant country, and even practiced a different religion. The man was Mahatma Gandhi, the great leader of India, who devoted his life to serving humanity in the spirit of love and nonviolence. It was in these principles that Martin discovered his method for social reform. More than anything else, those two principles were the key to his achievements.

This book is about black Americans who served society through the excellence of their achievements. It forms a part of the rich history of black men and women in America—a history of stunning accomplishments in every field of human endeavor, from literature and art to science, industry, education, diplomacy, athletics, jurisprudence, even polar exploration.

Not all of the people in this history had the same ideals, but I think you will find something that all of them have in common. Like Martin Luther King, Jr., they all decided to become "drum majors" and serve humanity. In that principle—whether it was expressed in books, inventions, or song—they found something outside themselves to use as a goal and a guide. Something that showed them a way to serve others, instead of living only for themselves.

Reading the stories of these courageous men and women not only helps us discover the principles that we will use to guide our own lives but also teaches us about our black heritage and about America itself. It is crucial for us to know the heroes and heroines of our history and to realize that the price we paid in our struggle for equality in America was dear. But we must also understand that we have gotten as far as we have partly because America's democratic system and ideals made it possible.

We are still struggling with racism and prejudice. But the great men and women in this series are a tribute to the spirit of our democratic ideals and the system in which they have flourished. And that makes their stories special and worth knowing.

JAMES
FARMER

1

PRISONER OF CONSCIENCE

───●◐●───

THE HINDS COUNTY Jail in Jackson, Mississippi, might very well have been the last place on earth a black man would look for liberty in 1961. Here in the heartland of Dixie, Confederate flags still aroused the passions of most of the white population, which continued to mourn the South's defeat in the Civil War—and the end of slavery—a century earlier. When Governor Ross Barnett shouted, "I love Mississippi!" at a 1961 football game, thousands of white fans knew he meant more than the indigenous mockingbirds and flowering magnolia trees—and they roared their approval for the traditions of white rule.

Nevertheless, James Farmer, locked in a cell in the Hinds County Jail, far from home and work on a Monday afternoon in June 1961, felt closer to freedom than ever before. To escape the stifling constraints of a town where blacks were treated as second-class citizens, he had left the Deep South of his childhood 2 decades earlier, at the age of 21. Farmer had headed north, intending to fight for the principles he believed in.

First in Chicago, then in New York City, he became a union organizer and civil rights activist, dedicating himself to the struggle against racial hate, injustice, bigotry, and exploitation. He worked to bring white and black Americans together as one people, firmly believing that as long as the races remained divided, racism would continue to flourish and blacks would continue to suffer.

Looking straight ahead, CORE leader James Farmer marches out of the Jackson, Mississippi, bus station after his 1961 arrest for violating state segregation laws. Farmer, along with a small group of fellow Freedom Riders, had courted police action by using facilities reserved for whites.

11

On May 24, 1961, just as Farmer went to jail in Mississippi, a new busload of Freedom Riders arrived in Montgomery, Alabama. Guarded by local police and Alabama National Guardsmen, this group included four white college professors and three black students.

In 1942, working with other committed men and women, Farmer founded the Committee of Racial Equality (CORE), an organization dedicated to ending discrimination against blacks. By 1961, CORE had attracted thousands of young people of all races, each of them committed to the fight against racism.

Buttressing the discrimination and segregation of the Deep South was not only custom but law. Farmer and his colleagues in the growing civil rights movement knew that before they could hope for true social justice in America, they would have to conquer the South. Thus it was that Farmer, at the age of 41, had returned to the hostile land of his youth. With him in 1961 was a small band of young people, all of them determined to break down the walls of prejudice between black and white Americans.

Arriving in Mississippi in Greyhound buses on May 24, the Freedom Riders—as Farmer and his young allies were called—brought their campaign to the Jackson bus station. Farmer and the other blacks marched into the whites-only waiting room, drank from the whites-only water fountain, then entered the whites-only restaurant. Meanwhile, white Freedom Riders took their places on the benches reserved for "colored." Both groups were deliberately violating the laws that prohibited the races to mingle in public places.

Ordered by the Jackson police to leave the bus station, the demonstrators refused. After arresting them for "disturbing the peace, disobeying an officer, and inciting to riot," the police herded the activists into patrol wagons and hauled them off to the Jackson City Jail. There, they refused orders to remain silent, roaring out hymns and freedom songs instead. Segregated even in prison, the Freedom Riders sang to each other through the echoing hallways. They were determined to fill the prisons of the South with their spirit as well as their bodies, overpowering the defenders of inequality with love and defiant nonviolence.

When the Jackson City Jail became too crowded, Farmer and the other Freedom Riders were moved to the Hinds County Jail. After a week behind bars, the riders heard a frightening rumor from other prisoners. Word was out, said the informants, that Farmer and his friends would soon be taken on an unscheduled leg of their Freedom Ride—to the dreaded Hinds County Prison Farm. Farmer noted that the men's voices dropped when they mentioned the prison farm; its treatment of black prisoners was notorious, even in Mississippi. "They're gonna whip yo' asses out there," Farmer remembered one man whispering. "Try to break you."

The next day, the Hinds County jailer appeared in front of Farmer's cell. A cold wave of fear passed though the prisoner; would it be now, he wondered, that he and his friends would be shackled together and sent to the farm? If so, the jailer gave no clue. Instead, he politely asked Farmer how the Freedom Riders were feeling. Well enough, replied Farmer, but they would feel better still if the state of Mississippi dropped the charges against them, released them from jail, and let them return to the bus station and sit where they liked. That way, said Farmer, he could call off other Freedom Rides in Mississippi, and the police could quit wasting their time arresting people for being in the wrong waiting room.

In Farmer's 1985 autobiography, *Lay Bare the Heart: An Autobiography of the Civil Rights Movement*, he recalled that the jailer sounded sad when he spoke. "Mr. Farmer, you know good'n well they ain't gonna to do that," he said softly. "Maybe when my grandchildren grow up, they'll do something like that. Lot 'a the young people down here don't feel like the old folks do; these things ain't goin' to go on forever. They cain't. Them boys with you is good boys. They ain't criminals. They hadn't oughta be in jail here. They ain't done nothing—they ain't killed nobody, or robbed, or raped. They just wanta be treated like everybody else."

The jailer, Farmer wrote later, lowered his eyes as he continued. "If I was a ni—if I was colored," he said, "I'd be doin' the same thing as them boys is. I understan' these boys. But," he added, gesturing toward the cells that held the white Freedom Riders, "I cain't understan' them white boys up there. They can go anywhere they wanna go; they're white. What they come down here for?"

"Well," replied Farmer, who had once planned to become a Methodist minister, "they believe, as Jesus

said, that all men are brothers." This simple idea was the only weapon that the Freedom Riders had brought to the fight against racial injustice. Their faith in the power of human kinship made them believe they could stand firm against any amount of brutality, hatred, and racism. "Black and white together," they sang at the top of their lungs. "We shall overcome," they sang, and they believed that they would.

The jailer, who knew that the Freedom Riders were headed for the prison farm, averted his eyes. His shoulders were shaking. The prisoner reached through the bars and patted his arm reassuringly. For Farmer, who fervently believed in the biblical ideal of loving one's enemy, it seemed as natural to

A pair of blood-spattered Freedom Riders, John Lewis (left) and James Zwerg, compare notes after being beaten by racists in Montgomery. Determined to end segregation, hundreds of volunteers followed Farmer's dangerous path through the Deep South.

comfort his oppressor as it was to seek freedom in a Mississippi jail. Unable to respond, the jailer slowly walked away.

Half an hour later, prison guards ordered the Freedom Riders into police vans and sent them to the Hinds County Prison Farm. For Farmer and his allies—and for the hundreds of civil rights volunteers

Max Thomas, superintendent of the Hinds County Prison Farm, directs Farmer and his friends toward the vans that will carry them to the penal farm. Although the CORE workers kept up a brave front, they had heard terrifying reports about the farm's sadistic, antiblack guards.

who would follow them—the path from the Jackson bus station to the town jail to the county jail to the county prison farm led to the last battle of the Civil War. It would be a battle fought with songs and clubs, with tear gas and hymns, with blind rage and calm faith. From it would emerge a new hero, a national leader in the struggle for freedom. ✿

2

A FAST LEARNER

JAMES LEONARD FARMER, Jr., was born in Marshall, Texas, on January 12, 1920. The second of Pearl and James Leonard Farmer, Sr.'s 3 children, he was just 17 months younger than his sister, Helen, but nearly 8 years older than his brother, Nathaniel. In spite of the difference in their ages, they all found it exceedingly difficult to escape from the tight grip of their domineering father.

"Being the son of a preacher does not really define my early childhood," James Farmer, Jr., wrote in *Lay Bare the Heart*. "Daddy was a minister, it is true, with all that implies. But he had another mystique."

Stern and strong willed, James, Sr., known to everybody as J. Leonard, had managed to acquire a first-rate education even though he came from humble beginnings. The son of impoverished former slaves, he finished grade school in Georgia, then worked his way through the Daytona Normal and Industrial Institute, the celebrated Florida school for blacks that educator Mary McLeod Bethune founded in 1904. Upon graduating from the Daytona Institute as an honors student, J. Leonard was so eager to continue his education that he walked all the way from Florida to Boston and enrolled in Boston University, which had accepted his application. He received top grades at this school, too, supporting himself as a valet and carriage boy while earning a Ph.D. in religion.

Three-year-old James Farmer displays his proudest possession outside his home in Holly Springs, Mississippi. James's father, J. Leonard Farmer, had moved his family to the small town when he took the jobs of dean, professor, and minister at the local black educational institution, Rust College.

J. Leonard Farmer subsequently returned to the South and married Pearl Houston, whom he had met at the Daytona Institute. The newlyweds settled in Texas, where he served for three years as minister of several small black Methodist churches. These posts left him feeling unfulfilled, however. The first black in the state's history to hold a doctorate—and perhaps the only Texan of any race who could read, write, and speak French and German as well as Hebrew, Greek, Aramaic, and Latin—he hungered for work that was more closely associated with academics.

J. Leonard Farmer finally received a position more to his liking in mid-1920, six months after the arrival of James, Jr. Accepting the job of dean, professor, and campus minister at Rust College, a black institution in the small Mississippi town of Holly Springs, James, Sr., moved his family to the tradition-steeped region known as the Bible Belt. The women in Holly Springs were so prim and proper that their skirts nearly touched their shoes, and the men behaved so rigidly that fundamentalist Christianity seemed to hang in the air.

Like his father, James, Jr., learned quickly; he could already read, write, and count by the time he entered the first grade. Bright, serious, and only four and a half years old, he quickly became a favorite of his teachers, who encouraged him to develop his intellect. Moreover, at school he met other gifted and privileged children, the offspring of Holly Springs's tiny elite of middle-class blacks.

As long as James stayed within the protective cocoon of the black college campus where he lived and attended elementary school, he felt secure. Sometimes, however, he caught a glimpse of the white-dominated world beyond the campus grounds. That was the case one hot summer day in 1923, when James was clinging to his mother's arm as she shopped in the town square. On the way home, the youngster looked up at her and said he wanted a soda.

"You can't get a Coke here, Junior," Pearl Farmer said, patting his sweating face with a snowy handkerchief. "Wait till we get home."

But James was thirsty, and he did not want to wait. He saw another boy go into a drugstore across the street, and he pulled his mother by her finger to look inside. Through the screen door, they could see the other boy sitting at the counter and sipping something cool. "See that, Mommy," James said. "We *can* get a Coke here."

"Son, I told you to wait till we get home. We *can't* get a Coke here."

"Then why could he?"

"He's white," his mother replied.

James did not understand. "He's white? And me?"

"You're colored."

James and his mother walked silently home along the red dirt road to the college, but he no longer held on to her. Nor did he want a soda anymore. When they got home, he just sat on the front porch, "a little brown boy alone with his three-and-a-half-year-old thoughts," as he put it later. His mother threw herself across her bed and cried, and his father came and sat by James without saying a word.

James was still too young to understand the things his father eventually tried to explain to him: that black Americans were outsiders even in their own hometown; that a white boy could walk into a downtown drugstore and buy a soda but that a black boy could not. Even later, when he did understand this state of affairs, James Farmer never learned to accept it. Long after he had grown into a man and begun to fight for equal rights for all, he would often dream of his introduction to racial discrimination. Each time, he would awaken as he heard his mother's words—"You're colored"—and feel his mind reel. There would be many more lessons in the harsh

Twenty-six years old when he sat for this portrait in 1913, J. Leonard Farmer had already earned one bachelor's degree in the arts and another in sacred theology. At this point, the brilliant young scholar was on his way toward earning his doctorate in religion from Boston University.

realities of racism and inequality, but for James Farmer, few would resound with such force.

When James was five years old, the Farmers moved again, this time to Austin, Texas, where his father had accepted the post of professor of religion and philosophy at Samuel Huston College. Like the town of Holly Springs, the city of Austin maintained separate worlds for its black and white residents. Austin's black district contained no paved roads and no sewers; the Farmers's one-story house had an outhouse instead of an indoor toilet. But the family always had enough food and clothing, and James never felt poor. After two years in Austin, the Farmers were able to afford a new car; on Sundays after church, they would drive out to visit friends in the country.

Coming home from such a visit late one afternoon, James's father hit a pig that was wandering on the road. He kept on driving. "Out in these rural parts," he told his wife, "Negroes are killed for less."

A few miles down the road, the family pulled over for a picnic supper of fried chicken and lemonade. As they began to eat, a pickup truck stopped, and two white men in overalls climbed out. One carried a shotgun.

J. Leonard jumped up and walked over to the men, with his son following closely. "You done kilt mah hawg, nigger," said the first man. "Y'all gon pay a purty penny fer that hawg."

James's father clutched his straw hat in his hand, and he looked down as he spoke. "I'm sorry, sir," he said, in a higher voice than usual. "If I killed your pig, I'll gladly pay for it. How much do you want for it?"

"That'll cost y'all $45, nigger," the man said. The elder Farmer produced his most recent paycheck—$57 for 2 weeks of work—endorsed it, and handed it over. The white man dropped the check. "Pick it up, nigger," he said.

James remembered hoping his father would refuse to retrieve it. J. Leonard, however, stooped to pick it up.

As they returned to their meal, father and son could not bear to look at each other. Meanwhile, James was making a silent vow. "I'll never do that when I grow up," he promised himself. "They'll have to kill me."

James could not reconcile the three very different faces his father wore at different times. To white people, he was a "good Negro," one who knew his "place." To black people, he was scholarly and impressive, a role model for other blacks struggling for recognition. To his children, he was both a deeply religious man and a stern disciplinarian.

Once, when James hit his sister, their father knocked him to the floor, whipped him with a belt, and then locked him in a closet. Could this be the same man who held James's hand and prayed with him when Nathaniel nearly died of pneumonia? Was it the same man who allowed whites to treat him like a wayward child? James would take from his father a lifelong burning commitment to moral principles. He would also take a deep revulsion for the kind of hypocrisy he sensed in his father's varying personality.

Puzzled by his father's multiple faces, James was also baffled by the fact that he himself seemed to be a different person in different circumstances. In school with other black students, James ran into few problems. He was easily the smartest in his class, and although he did not study much, he could always answer questions that stumped his classmates. Futhermore, nobody picked on him. He was not a fighter, but he could always count on a brawny classmate to defend him in return for assistance with homework. To cap off James's self-confidence, his best friend was the principal's son.

But in the mysterious and menacing white sec-

James and his big sister, Helen, join their mother, Pearl, for a family album shot in the summer of 1924. Pearl Houston had met J. Leonard Farmer in 1916, when both were students at the Daytona Normal and Industrial Institute, Mary McLeod Bethune's pioneering Florida school for blacks.

His expression unnoticed by his stern father, five-year-old James Farmer mugs for the camera as he and Helen pose for a 1925 picture. "Daddy was a minister," James wrote later, "with all that implies."

tions of Austin—a world so close and yet so far beyond his grasp—James felt his customary defenses slip away. While he was in high school, he got a job as a golf caddy at the local country club. Soon after he began work, he made the mistake of sitting on the wrong bench. No sign identified it as reserved for white caddies only, but the boys who had worked at the club longer than James understood the unwritten rule.

Deciding to give James a pointed lesson in racial etiquette, a white boy slid over and began to elbow him sharply in the ribs. James's muscular school friend, Nelson, who also worked as a caddy, came to his rescue by taking over James's seat and then beating the white boy in a wrestling match. The defeated caddy drew a knife, but he was quickly disarmed by his white friends. James was prepared to forget the incident, but, he reported later, when his father heard about it, James's "caddying career came to a screeching halt." As far as J. Leonard Farmer was concerned, the best way to deal with most whites was not at all.

His father, noted James, tried to make the most of his position as a "good Negro" and a respected scholar. But there were limits to what even a prominent middle-class black man could expect in Austin. As an adult, James Farmer would remember thinking that his father spent much of his energy placating Austin's white community.

One year, for example, the senior Farmer went down to the railroad station to reserve train tickets to New York for his sister-in-law and her husband, who had been visiting James and his family in Austin. The New York couple had traveled south in a Pullman train car and had slept in their own bedroom compartment. J. Leonard knew it would not be so easy to book similar accommodations out of Austin. There, luxuries such as bedroom compartments were reserved for whites only.

Accompanying his father to the train depot, James heard him tell train officials—untruthfully—that his brother-in-law was a newspaper editor hurrying north for an urgent meeting. Such an important person, suggested J. Leonard, deserved a bedroom, even if he *was* black. The officials agreed but required the couple to sneak onto the train under cover of darkness so Austin residents would not see them. It was the kind of compromise with discrimination that James Farmer, Jr., would come to abhor with all his soul.

By the time he was in his early teens, James could hardly wait to escape his father's make-do universe, which he later described as "the squeezing of one's soul into a room too small." He felt a battle between two natures taking place inside himself: One was gentle, submissive, polite, polished, and studious; the other, angry, rebellious, and increasingly resentful of having to swallow his pride and principles in order to get along. James Farmer's internal struggle between compromise and revolt would form the major conflict of his life, flaring up repeatedly in battles large and small, public and private, always rumbling beneath the surface when things seemed most calm.

Despite his self-doubts and inner turmoil, James sailed quickly and easily through school, skipping grades and earning praise as a sharp thinker and a forceful speaker. When he was 12 years old, he received a full 4-year college scholarship as a reward for winning a series of high school oratorical contests.

At the age of 14, slim and 6 feet tall, James was ready for college. By this time, he knew he could succeed; as a gifted student from a comparatively comfortable home, he held great advantages over most blacks his age. But what kind of success would he use his gifts to attain? Would he try to be the best at the same game everyone else was playing? Or would he try to change the game itself? ⟐

3

JESUS AND JIM CROW

James Farmer was only 14 years old when he graduated from high school and entered Wiley College in Marshall, Texas. An outstanding student, the poised, six-foot-tall youngster was already noted as a highly skilled speechmaker; it was a talent that would serve him well in later years.

IN THE FALL of 1934, J. Leonard and James Farmer headed for Marshall, Texas, the father to teach at Wiley College, the son to enroll as a freshman. Ironically, James Farmer would reach maturity by returning to the town of his birth and achieve independence by going there with the one person he was determined to break away from.

By this time, Marshall's population had grown to 18,000. Some of the town's blacks had gained the respect of their white neighbors, but even the most prominent black citizens had to humble themselves before Jim Crow. Originating in minstrel shows, the popular blackface musicals of the late 19th and early 20th centuries, the term *Jim Crow* had come to mean racial discrimination.

It was Jim Crow laws that assigned blacks to inferior schools and seats at the back of buses and trains; Jim Crow regulations that made it harder for blacks to vote than whites; Jim Crow employment practices that assigned blacks to the most menial jobs; Jim Crow customs that called for blacks to accept white rudeness or mistreatment without complaint.

The U.S. Supreme Court, in a historic 1896 decision, had declared that blacks could be legally segregated as long as their facilities were "equal." In fact, however, Jim Crow's separate hospitals, separate beaches, separate drinking fountains, separate toilets, separate waiting rooms, separate theater seats were almost never equal, particularly in the South.

In Marshall, Texas, no black, not even the president of Wiley College, was allowed to enter a downtown department store and try on a suit. If a black man wanted to take his family out to dinner, he took them to a "colored" restaurant; if they wanted to see a movie, they watched it from "nigger heaven," a separate section at the back of the top balcony. When they went to church, they went to a black church. Even in death, Jim Crow ruled the South; blacks were laid to rest in strictly segregated grave-yards.

Jim Crow, of course, was an old acquaintance of James Farmer's; segregation in Marshall was no different than segregation in Holly Springs or segregation in Austin. But Wiley College, segregated though it was, was different. The small college, with its ivy-covered buildings, excellent faculty, and diverse student body, provided a world of its own, a place where each individual had a chance to grow and develop his or her own gifts. It was exactly what the 14-year-old Farmer, hungry for intellectual challenge, needed. He blossomed at Wiley.

Not only in the classroom, but outside it, Farmer seized every chance to use and expand his natural abilities. He served as president of his fraternity, captain of the college debating team, chairman of the drama and chemistry clubs, Methodist church youth leader, and senior class president.

Poet and English professor Melvin B. Tolson, who was also coach of the debating team, became Farmer's mentor at Wiley. He forced his young protégé to work harder than he ever had in his life, not only exploring new intellectual territory but reexamining his most deeply held beliefs. Paying tribute to his idol many years later, Farmer said that Tolson "stretched the minds of all whose minds would be stretched." Several nights each week, Farmer joined other students in lively debates and discussions at Tolson's home. Tolson sometimes read his own work to the students, sparking visions of a promised land with his poems about Harlem, New York City's fabled black community.

Newly aware of the power of his own intellect, Farmer savored the challenge of dueling with others, of scoring victories with the sheer force of superior logic. In his autobiography, he recalled a night when he and a friend sat up until dawn discussing the absurdity of racial segregation. By the time they finished their impassioned dialogue, Farmer later told Tolson, the two young men had destroyed segregation once and for all—verbally, at least. Listening to Farmer's enthusiastic report, Tolson seemed to smile and frown at the same time.

"I hear there was a good movie showing downtown Saturday, a Hollywood extravaganza," Tolson said to Farmer. "Did you see it?"

Farmer said he had seen the movie and very much enjoyed it.

"Where did you sit?" asked Tolson.

"In the balcony, of course, where we always sit," replied Farmer.

"The other night, you damned segregation to hell," said Tolson. "Then on Saturday, in the pitiless glare of the sun, you walked downtown to the Paramount Theater, went around to the side entrance, climbed the back stairs, sat in the buzzards' roost, and enjoyed the movie. You hate segregation, but you've paid your father's hard-earned money for the privilege of being segregated."

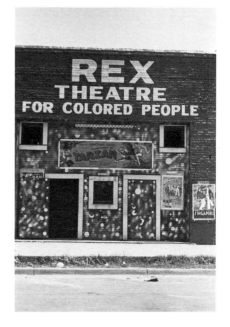

Until the civil rights movement of the 1960s changed the face of the South, black southerners watched movies in all-black theaters such as this one or from the top-balcony seats that whites called "nigger heaven." As a college student, Farmer began reordering his values when he realized he had always accepted such segregation without question.

Suddenly aware of his own self-contradictory behavior—unprotestingly joining the system he opposed so deeply—Farmer for once found himself speechless. In light of his actions, all his elegant arguments seemed meaningless. He realized Tolson was right: How could he defeat Jim Crow when he allowed it to dictate where he sat for a movie? To further stimulate Farmer's now-aroused consciousness, Tolson gave him an essay to read: "Civil Disobedience," in which American philosopher Henry David Thoreau recommends refusing to obey laws that conflict with one's sense of justice and righteousness.

The professor also gave Farmer some parting advice: "My boy, it's customary for a professor to tell his students that the world is waiting for them with open arms," he said. "Well, that's a lie. There are men waiting for you, all right—with a big stick. Learn how to duck, and counterpunch."

Farmer began to look more critically at the day-to-day realities for blacks in Marshall, Texas. Segregation and other forms of racial discrimination were unquestionable facts of life there. Open to question, however, was the matter of responsibility. By going along with segregation, were blacks helping strengthen it? Could they oppose racism and appease it at the same time? Farmer began to examine his own position. Unless he made his life an example of his ideals, he asked himself, what were his ideals really worth?

He soon found an opportunity to answer some of his own questions. As president of Omega Psi Phi fraternity during his senior year, he got caught up in a petty rivalry among the campus fraternities and sororities over who would choose the homecoming queen. The trivial dispute assumed absurdly large proportions, and Farmer saw members of his own fraternity growing increasingly hostile to members of other Greek-letter societies. The homecoming-queen issue had become the chief topic of debate on campus.

Farmer was dismayed by the sight of black students dividing over such a meaningless issue, and he was disgusted with himself for taking part. As it turned out, his opposite number—the president of his fraternity's chief rival—felt the same way. After comparing notes, the two young men decided to quit their fraternities and form a new association, dedicated to eliminating all fraternities and sororities from Wiley.

Making speeches and nailing up handbills on the campus bulletin board, the former rivals denounced fraternities and sororities as elitist, divisive, and bad for black people. If black students were torn apart by rivalries, Farmer and his friend argued, they would never be able to unite against their common enemy—racism. The young men failed in their campaign, but from it Farmer took valuable lessons in the arts of persuasion and publicity.

Inevitably, Farmer began to wonder what he should do with the lessons he was learning. "My ambition was to wage war on racism," he recalled later, "but how would I earn a living?" He considered becoming a doctor, but when he discovered that the sight of blood made him ill, he dropped the idea. "It did not occur to me that in the civil rights struggle I would see more blood than I ever would have seen in a doctor's office or a hospital operating room," he noted wryly.

In the end, Farmer found himself following in his father's footsteps, toward the ministry. He joined and eventually became the leader of the Methodist youth association at Wiley. Representing his college at the 1937 National Conference of Methodist Youth, held in Oxford, Ohio, he urged his fellow delegates to take a strong position on public issues and to make

Howard University professor Howard Thurman introduced Farmer to the ideas of Mohandas K. Gandhi, the Indian philosopher and political activist who preached and practiced the tactics of nonviolent direct action. Deeply impressed, Farmer would strive to follow the Gandhian way for the rest of his life.

their voice heard. To begin with, Farmer proposed that the conference should call on the U.S. Congress to make lynching a federal crime.

For decades, most lynchings went unchallenged throughout much of the United States. In the decade ending in 1920, the year of Farmer's birth, for instance, lynch mobs murdered nearly 900 black men and women. Most of these lynchings occurred in the South, but no state in the Union offered complete safety for blacks; mob murders took place in Pennsylvania, Michigan, and Nebraska as well as in Georgia, Texas, and South Carolina.

Official lynching statistics—which probably reveal only a portion of the actual extralegal executions committed in the United States—indicate that, between the years 1882 and 1968, 3,446 blacks met death at the hands of mobs. Not only incomplete, this figure fails to account for the atmosphere of terror and intimidation that lynching created for blacks: At any time, blacks whose behavior displeased the white community might find themselves the prey of the Ku Klux Klan or other racist groups.

Almost as astonishing as the number of lynchings is the fact that most of these crimes had the unspoken consent of the law. Lynchers were rarely accused or brought to trial; when they were, they were almost always acquitted. Indeed, unless they carried their victims across state lines, lynchers violated no federal law. Lynching was murder, a crime that fell (as it still does) under state, not federal, jurisdiction.

Decade after decade, civil rights activists, including the intrepid Walter White of the National Association for the Advancement of Colored People (NAACP), campaigned for federal legislation against lynching; decade after decade, such legislation was torpedoed by southern senators, who claimed the threat of lynching was necessary to keep blacks "in line." Despite this history of frustration, Farmer, already displaying the deep-voiced eloquence that would gain him acclaim as a civil rights leader, persuaded the Young Methodist Youth Conference to pass his resolution. It had no more effect on the South's implacable opposition to antilynching laws than earlier efforts, but, like the fraternity battle, it helped shape a uniquely effective leader.

When the 18-year-old Farmer graduated from Wiley in 1938, he once more followed his father's footsteps, this time to Washington, D.C. When J. Leonard Farmer accepted a position teaching Greek at the Howard University School of Religion, the family moved to the capital, and James began studying for the ministry.

Farmer's years at Howard coincided with a golden age for the predominantly black university, which had been founded in 1867 to educate recently freed black men. Howard—which later accepted students of both sexes and all races—had become one of the nation's most prestigious colleges; its graduates included some of the nation's leading clerics, doctors, lawyers, engineers, and architects.

Farmer soon discovered that Jim Crow controlled the nation's capital as surely as he did any town in the Deep South. Across the city, strict segregation prevailed in residential districts, department stores, waiting rooms, movie theaters, schools, hospitals, and public transportation. For Farmer, helping to counteract Washington, D.C.'s disillusioning bigotry was the atmosphere of America's "black Athens," Howard University. Among the brilliant scholars then attached to the school were philosopher Alain Locke, political scientist Ralph Bunche, legal authority William Hastie, and writer Sterling Brown.

Even more important to Farmer, of course, was the faculty at Howard's divinity school. The young graduate student found himself especially impressed by Howard Thurman, a renowned philosopher, poet,

Farmer spent countless hours studying in the Carnegie Library at Howard University, which he entered in 1938. While he was enrolled at the prestigious Washington, D.C., college, Farmer became a student secretary for the antiviolence Fellowship of Reconciliation (FOR), thereby taking the first step toward his life's work.

Refused entry to an all-white church in St. Augustine, Florida, in 1964, three black Methodists keep a silent vigil outside. More than 20 years earlier, segregation within the Methodist denomination had prompted Farmer to refuse ordination as a minister. Some American Christians, he suggested, thought J.C. stood for Jim Crow, not Jesus Christ.

and preacher who focused on expanding students' souls as much as their minds.

Thurman introduced Farmer to the teachings of Mohandas K. Gandhi, the great Indian leader who had led a nonviolent but eventually successful revolt against British rule in India. Gandhi's profound spiritual faith and his understanding of how to harness the strength of an oppressed people, without taking up arms against the oppressor, greatly influenced Farmer, who was searching for solutions to his own people's oppression.

During his years at Howard, Farmer became a student secretary for the Fellowship of Reconciliation (FOR), a national organization of some 12,000

people committed to pacifism. Like others in the
FOR, Farmer opposed all violence; even in the midst
of war, he believed, killing a human being was
wrong. FOR members were dedicated to the search
for alternative ways to resolve people's differences
peacefully. Like Farmer, many hoped to follow Gandhi's example, achieving social change in America
without the use of violence.

In early 1941, the 21-year-old Farmer became
national chairman of the Youth Committee Against
War, a group of young people strenuously opposed to
America's entry into World War II. As the United
States moved ever closer to joining the global conflict, Eleanor Roosevelt, wife of President Franklin
D. Roosevelt, invited Farmer and 30 other national
youth leaders to visit the White House and discuss
"matters of mutual concern" with herself and the
president.

Farmer, the only black in the group, found
himself sharing a small table with the president's
wife, a tall, gracious woman known for her sensitivity
to human rights. During dinner, she listened atten-
tively to Farmer's ideas, earning the awed admiration
of the intense young student. "I was being accepted
as a peer," he recalled, "by a person of supreme
importance in the scale of things: the wife of the
most powerful man in the world."

After dinner, the president displayed his leg-
endary charm and grace as he addressed the group.
The war in Europe, he said, was the final struggle
between good and evil. The United States was
morally obliged to come to the aid of France and
Great Britain, which were defending democracy
against the aggressive dictatorship of Adolf Hitler's
Nazi Germany.

As the president spoke, Farmer thought of Africa,
from which his ancestors had been taken as slaves.
He knew that large parts of the continent were still

ruled, against the will of the black Africans, by the
countries Roosevelt embraced as allies. When the
president finished his talk and asked for questions,
many hands shot up. Roosevelt called first on the
only black in the room.

"Mr. President," Farmer said, "in your opening
remarks you described Britain and France as champi-
ons of freedom. In light of their colonial policies in
Africa, which give the lie to that principle, how can
they still be considered its defenders?"

The smile dropped from the president's face. He
stared at the ceiling for a few moments, then pointed
his slender cigarette holder at Farmer. "Let's not put
it that way," Roosevelt said. "Let's put it this way. In
which country would *you* rather live today—France
or Nazi Germany?" His smile returned.

Before Farmer had a chance to reply, Eleanor
Roosevelt rose and addressed her husband. "Just a
minute," she said. "You did *not* answer the question!"

Roosevelt lit another cigarette, then replied to
his wife. "The question was this: Why do I consider
Britain and France to be more on the side of freedom
than Nazi Germany, despite their colonization laws?
And I answered it thus. You will please let *me* handle
the questions!"

The president had indicated why he favored
Britain and France over Germany, but he had not
answered the question that troubled Farmer: How
could the United States and its allies justify fighting
for freedom abroad while they continued to deny true
freedom to many of the people under their gover-
nance? Farmer left the White House with the growing
sense that ideas and actions were very different things
and that actions meant far more.

Farmer felt frustrated by the great distance between what was preached and what was practiced,
not only in the White House, but in the church he
was preparing to serve as a minister. Jim Crow might

not speak from the pulpit, but, Farmer observed, Jim Crow sat in the pews. Black Methodists and white Methodists each had their own "jurisdiction," based not on where they lived or what they believed but on the color of their skin.

For Farmer, segregation in his own church posed a fundamental challenge to his most heartfelt beliefs. Haunted by the way the church could serve as a cloak for injustice, he chose to write his final thesis at Howard University on the relationship between religion and racism. In his paper, Farmer argued that historically, organized religion had tended to bolster the racial notions held by whatever group was dominant in society at the time. Some Protestant teachings, he pointed out, had been used by Europeans to justify the colonization, exploitation, and enslavement of people with dark skin. In the United States, Farmer seemed to suggest, Jesus Christ had been made into a mouthpiece for Jim Crow.

Such views clearly put Farmer at odds with his church. In May 1941, as he prepared to graduate from the Howard University School of Religion, he told his father he had decided not to be ordained a Methodist minister. To James's surprised relief, J. Leonard Farmer took the news calmly. "After reading your excellent thesis," he said to his son, "I understand. I know that whatever you do, you'll do well, but what *are* you going to do?"

"Destroy segregation," said James Farmer. ✢

4

THE NEW BROTHERHOOD

WHEN JAMES FARMER told his father that he planned to "destroy segregation," the older man responded with a quite natural question: "How?" Although the 21-year-old divinity school graduate had no specific answer at the moment—"It'll have something to do with mass mobilization and the use of the Gandhi technique," he had replied—a practical answer soon materialized. It came in the form of a telephone call from the New York City headquarters of the Fellowship of Reconciliation.

Would Farmer be interested, asked an FOR executive, in remaining with the organization after college? Of course! said Farmer; if possible, he added, he would like "something in the field of race." Obligingly appointing Farmer race relations secretary, a $15-per-week job that involved making speeches about pacifism, the FOR sent him to Chicago.

Farmer, who had never before been far away from home, was awed by the vast Illinois metropolis—this "rip-snorting behemoth," he called Chicago—with its immense lake, roaring elevated trains, and towering business district. At the same time, he was depressed and angered by the city's rotting, miserable slums, where its black population dwelled in shadowy poverty. During the first months after his move,

Residents of Chicago's notorious South Side gaze from their tenement's dilapidated wooden fire escapes in 1941. Arriving that year in the Illinois metropolis, Farmer was excited by its cosmopolitan atmosphere but appalled by its wretched slums.

39

however, he spent less time in Chicago than in Cleveland, Milwaukee, Indianapolis, and the other midwestern cities where he delivered antiwar speeches.

The FOR had opposed war for decades, most of them periods of relative peace for the United States. As the nation edged closer to entering World War II, the organization stepped up its campaign of opposition, and when Congress declared war—following the December 7, 1941, Japanese attack on the U.S. naval base at Pearl Harbor, Hawaii—the FOR was ready. Its plans included encouraging young men to refuse to fight if they were drafted into military service and assisting those whose refusal brought government retribution.

Farmer, who wholeheartedly agreed with the FOR's view of war as mass murder, had a second objection to joining the military: He believed that the racially segregated armed forces betrayed the ideals of freedom and equality for which they were fighting. Prepared to go to jail rather than serve, he filled out a form for conscientious objectors and brought it with him to his draft board.

Farmer expected a battle in winning exemption from military service, but not the kind he encountered. "You're a minister of the gospel," the draft board chairman told him. "You can't be a conscientious objector."

"But I *am* a conscientious objector to war," insisted Farmer.

The man was immovable: "As far as we're concerned, you're a minister." And on those grounds—rather than on Farmer's deep-seated objections to war—the official said that his military service would be deferred. Farmer left the interview with mixed feelings: guilt, in that he had avoided the draft for the wrong reason, and joy, in that he was now free to work on his campaign against discrimination. When

he told his father about his experience with the draft board, the older man smiled. "I have a feeling, Junior," he said, "that the chairman and some members of his board thought you could fight better at home than abroad."

Indeed, Farmer had already given a name to his program for breaking down the barriers between the races and for dismantling legal discrimination against black Americans. "With all the pretentiousness of youth," he recalled later, he had sat down at his kitchen table and had written on a yellow legal pad a document he called "A Provisional Plan for Brotherhood Mobilization."

After studying the nonviolent techniques that Gandhi had used to gain India's freedom, Farmer envisioned a similar mass movement in the United States, this one targeting discrimination. Unlike earlier organized efforts to achieve justice for black Americans, such as the NAACP and the National

Union organizer and civil rights champion A. Philip Randolph leads a group of Pennsylvanians protesting military segregation in the 1940s. Farmer, both committed to pacifism and strongly opposed to racial segregation, was ready to go to prison rather than serve in the armed forces.

Urban League, Farmer's movement would emphasize "an army of ground troops" rather than an "elegant cadre of generals." He envisioned the brotherhood "beginning with FOR members, then broadening its base and becoming a mass movement, filling up the jails if necessary."

The key to Farmer's movement was action. "Segregation will go on as long as we permit it to," he wrote. "We must withhold our support and participation from . . . segregation in every area of American life." Like Gandhi, Farmer championed civil disobedience—the peaceable refusal to obey unjust laws—and "jail where necessary." Emulating Gandhi's followers, Farmer's civil rights volunteers would never resort to violence, but neither would they shy away from active resistance to the laws and policies they sought to change.

"The movement," wrote Farmer, "must have a distinctive and radical approach. It must strive . . . not to make housing in ghettos more tolerable, but to destroy residential segregation; not to make Jim Crow facilities the equal of others, but to abolish Jim Crow; not to make racial discrimination more bearable, but to wipe it out. . . . We must not stop until racial brotherhood is established in the United States as a fact as well as an ideal."

Farmer, in other words, was advocating specific action: Blacks should understand, once and for all, that *separate but equal* was a self-contradictory term, that separate facilities were never equal. Blacks, Farmer was saying, must refuse to accept anything but the *same* facilities as whites, fighting for them if necessary.

Confident that FOR director A. J. Muste would share his enthusiasm, Farmer sent him a copy of the new Brotherhood program. While he waited for Muste's response, Farmer turned his attention to an entirely new occupation: being in love.

Farmer took one look at 20-year-old drugstore clerk Winnie Christie (pictured here at the age of 21) and fell hopelessly in love. Rapturously, he described her as a "composite of all my favorite movie actresses" and a "mixture of all my love fantasies wrapped in a coffee-with-cream skin."

Several years younger than his college classmates, Farmer had been more comfortable with philosophy than romance. He had never had a girlfriend. But all that changed one day in 1941, when he walked into Chicago's Bronzeville Drugstore and ordered a White Owl cigar. Behind the cigar counter stood a smashingly beautiful young woman, her olive-skinned face framed by long braids, her smile quizzical, her manner reserved but pleasant.

One glance from Winnie Christie's "langorous" eyes, Farmer said later, "stopped me in midsentence, openmouthed." Unable to get her off his mind, he returned to the store day after day, buying more cigars and chewing gum than he could ever use and trying to raise the courage to ask Christie to have dinner with him. When he finally did it, she amazed and delighted him by saying yes at once. The couple's mutual attraction quickly turned to love. Their fragile, passionate romance would be among the most intense emotional experiences of James Farmer's long life.

Not entirely blinded by love, Farmer continued to follow his star, the quest for racial equality. That winter, he took part in an interracial housing action, engaged in what may have been the nation's first restaurant sit-in, and assailed the discriminatory policy of a popular entertainment center.

The housing experiment began with an invitation from James Robinson, a white graduate student at the University of Chicago. Impressed by Farmer's Brotherhood Mobilization proposal—which had been printed and circulated among the city's reform-minded young people—Robinson asked him to help establish Boys' Fellowship House, a racially mixed residence that would challenge the legality of the city's segregated housing. Farmer, of course, leapt at the offer.

With a few white friends, Robinson rented a large house on the white side of the border between black and white Chicago. The building was bound by a document in which the landlord swore to sell or rent his or her property to whites only. It was common practice for property owners of entire neighborhoods to sign these documents, known as restrictive covenants, which made it virtually impossible for black tenants to find decent housing. Even though Robinson and his friends had not signed such an agreement, the owner of the house had assumed she was renting it to white tenants only. She had a surprise in store: Farmer moved in at once.

As soon as the landlord learned that her new tenants included a nonwhite, her lawyer ordered the young men to get out at once or face serious legal action. They shot back a reply, asserting that they had signed a valid lease and had no intention of leaving. In any event, the opportunity to argue in court for integration was exactly what they wanted.

They did not get their day in court. The terms of the lease ran only for six months, and the landlord decided to wait it out rather than try to evict the integrationists. Undaunted, the young people then rented a large apartment in another all-white neighborhood. One month later, the inevitable letter arrived: "We are advised that there are in residence," it said, "persons other than those of you who signed the lease, and that among those persons are non-Caucasians, constituting a great source of annoyance to the neighbors."

The landlord, a large real estate company, ordered Farmer and his friends to leave; instead, they took a neighborhood poll. Calling at every apartment on their block, they asked if anyone objected to their presence. "The answer was no," Farmer recalled. "Most said we were good neighbors . . . [and] many signed statements in our support."

This time, the case went to court. Farmer and his friends showed up with statements in hand. Astonished by the group's careful preparation, the landlord's lawyers immediately asked for a postponement of the case. "Unable to scare us out," remarked Farmer, "this landlord was no more anxious than the previous one had been to risk a court case on housing bias." After two years of postponements, the landlord dropped the case.

Restrictive covenants would remain in legal use until 1948. In that year, a team of lawyers from the NAACP would manage to take a covenant case all the way to the U.S. Supreme Court, which ruled the practice unconstitutional. Largely the work of the NAACP's brilliant attorney Thurgood Marshall, the landmark covenant victory was made possible, as Marshall and his aides well knew, by the groundwork of Farmer, Robinson, and other dedicated and persistent young men and women.

While they were engaged in their open-housing action, Farmer and Robinson began meeting on Saturday afternoons with a small, racially mixed

Nationalist and spiritual leader Mohandas K. Gandhi urged his fellow Indians not to take up arms against the British occupiers of their country but to practice massive civil disobedience, a strategy that eventually brought India its freedom. Farmer had no doubt that Gandhi's methods would work equally well in freeing black America from racist laws and customs.

group of graduate students who agreed that racial injustice could best be overcome by nonviolent protest. Together, the young people pored over *War Without Violence*, a book about nonviolent resistance by Krishnalal Shridharani, a disciple of Gandhi's.

Like Shridharani, the Chicago students were drawn to the concept of *satyagraha*, which means, roughly, "the firmness engendered by love." They, too, felt that love was the strongest weapon against hate and that they should seek to reason with their foes, not fight them. The group, recalled Farmer, "believed that truth alone, the transparent justice of our demands, would convert the segregationists, once they agreed to listen."

After studying Shridharani's explanation of Gandhi's techniques for dismantling an unjust system without bloodshed or hatred, the group designed its own four-step system to deal with each case: First, investigate to uncover the facts; second, negotiate and try to persuade those in charge to change their policies; third (if the first two steps fail), publicize the protest, seeking to win public support; fourth (if nothing else brings change), deliberately violate the wrongful policies and be prepared to accept the consequences.

Farmer's group soon found an opportunity to start practicing Gandhi's system. Deciding to go out for coffee after a meeting one snowy evening, Farmer and Robinson headed for the nearby Jack Spratt Coffee House. The two young men sat at the counter, deep in the conversation they had started on the way over. At last, Farmer, feeling a chill, looked up. "The manager of the Jack Spratt Coffee House," he recalled, "was standing right over me, looking meanly into my face."

"You'll have to get out of here," hissed the manager. "We can't serve you here."

Farmer had known these words would be spoken. "I had intellectualized a thousand answers that would

destroy dragons and reduce that little man to ashes,"
he recalled. Nevertheless, when the moment arrived,
he found himself almost speechless. Robinson, his
face bright red but his voice steady, saved the day. "I
suppose you realize that there is a civil rights law in
this state forbidding this kind of practice," he said to
the manager. "Now if you don't serve us, I promise
that you're going to pay the stiffest penalty the law
allows."

The manager grudgingly complied, but Farmer
and Robinson decided they "owed it to that man's
religion to return to his place of business," and return
they did. This time, they brought a half-dozen other
black and white friends, including Winnie Christie,
Farmer's new girlfriend. Unhappy about going where
she was "not wanted," Christie came reluctantly.
Farmer knew his world of "fierce-eyed young activist
radicals" was not her world, but he was determined to
share it with her. He hoped she would sense some of
the excitement he felt at starting a social revolution.

Before they had left Boys' Fellowship House for
the coffee shop, Farmer had briefed his friends. They
would be peaceful and orderly, and they would
remain calm, smiling as much as possible. White and
black members of the group would sit together;
whites would not eat unless the blacks were served as
well. As they started off for the restaurant, Farmer
recalled, he had felt "a delicious tension," as though
he were the lead actor in a Broadway play on opening
night.

The Jack Spratt manager at first ignored the
group, then sullenly told his staff to go ahead and
serve them. But after they had eaten, paid, and left,
he ran after them and hurled their payment to the
ground. "Take your money and get out of here!" he
screamed. The group, newly baptized in the gospel of
nonviolent activism, left the cash lying in the street
so they could not be accused of leaving their bill
unpaid.

Step one, investigation, had been completed. It was now clear that blacks would be treated with hostility at Jack Spratt. For step two, negotiation, Farmer called the restaurant to ask for a meeting to discuss the issue. The manager hung up on him. Farmer then wrote to request a conference.

While he waited for the manager's answer—which would never come—Farmer got a letter from Winnie Christie. "Jim, darling," it said in part, "it breaks my heart to tell you, we live in different worlds. . . . I love you so much that it hurts. I want to help you but I can't, and I would never want to hold you back." Farmer tried desperately to reach his sweetheart, but she had disappeared. "I cried," he wrote later. "I'm sure the only antidote for a heart that hurts . . . is to submerge oneself in work."

Receiving no response to Farmer's letter, the group sent several members to the coffee shop, but the management refused to budge. At last, one sunny day in May 1942, the sit-in was born at Jack Spratt. Led by Farmer, 28 men and women, black and white, walked into the coffee shop and occupied every available seat. When the restaurant's other patrons, all of them white, noticed that waitresses were not serving the black customers, many stopped eating. Some passed their food on to blacks sitting near them. Others, recalled Farmer, stopped eating because "they did not want to miss any of this drama."

Confronted by a restaurant full of people eating nothing, the irate day manager called the police. "I want you to throw these people out," she told the two patrolmen who arrived on the scene.

"What're they doing wrong?" asked one of the policemen. "You're open for business, aren't you? They're not trespassing."

With that, recalled Farmer, "The cops left, one winking at me as he passed by."

Dejectedly, the manager ordered the staff to serve everyone. Farmer and his allies finished their meals, paid their bills, and exited. This time, no one threw their money after them.

The next day, Robinson wrote Jack Spratt, thanking the shop for its fine service and offering congratulations on its change of policy. This letter received no response either. But from that point on, the restaurant served all races without incident.

In 1942, in the midst of World War II, the integration of Chicago's Jack Spratt Coffee House caused no national—or even local—headlines. But the event, the staging of the nation's first organized civil rights sit-in, looms large in American social history. Civil rights activists, James Farmer among them, would use the same nonviolent direct-action tactics some two decades later to hammer the final nail into Jim Crow's coffin. ❧

HE DRAFT BOARDS
DID NOT
XCLUDE NEGROES
CITY
G RINK
ASH
BEFORE
SMASHE
IKE A BLO
AT
D JIM CRO
WHITE CITY
DEFIES
BILL OF RIGHTS
PICK

5

THE BIRTH OF CORE

ACROSS THE RACIAL divide, in black Chicago, another building caught the attention of James Farmer's integration team in 1942. A white eight-foot-high wall with an iron gate separated an immense white brick structure from the surrounding ghetto. Inside the castlelike building was a roller skating rink that admitted white skaters only. The rink was aptly named White City.

Several black members of Farmer's integration team tried to gain admission to the rink but were turned away. Twelve white members of the group followed them to the ticket window; unlike their friends, they were permitted to buy tickets and were admitted promptly. Yet when Farmer tried to purchase an admission ticket, the ticket seller told him the rink had been reserved for a private party and was closed to the general public.

"One has to be a member of some unnamed private club to skate tonight. Is that correct?" Farmer asked.

"That is right."

"Then why is it," Farmer wanted to know, "that twelve of my friends are in there skating and are not members of any private club and have no membership cards?" On cue, two of his white friends appeared inside the doorway to expose the White City Roller Skating Rink in its lie: The private party was being given by Jim Crow.

CORE members block the path of would-be ticket purchasers at the entrance to Chicago's segregated White City Roller Skating Rink. Started by Farmer in 1942, CORE's campaign against the rink's whites-only policy lasted four years; White City finally admitted black skaters in 1946.

51

The next morning, Farmer's group swore out complaints against the White City management and had the rink's manager, ticket seller, and ticket taker arrested for practicing racial discrimination. Then, as a gesture of goodwill, Farmer and his friends paid the offenders' bail. Neither action persuaded the White City management to stop excluding blacks, so the integrationists tried a different tactic. Every night for the next several months, they returned to the rink and tied up the admission line with interracial groups trying to gain entrance, thus seriously undercutting the rink's ability to turn a profit.

In April 1942, as the skating rink dispute simmered, the National Council of the FOR met in Columbus, Ohio. Among the topics that came under discussion was Farmer's "Provisional Plan for Brotherhood Mobilization"; he wanted permission to establish "an army of ground troops" within the FOR. Addressing the 40 members of the council, he confidently explained that segregation would end only when "people withdraw their cooperation from it and stop, wittingly or unwittingly, giving it their support." To achieve that goal, Farmer asked for the council's backing "in setting up a vehicle through which that noncooperation with evil can be forged into a national movement."

Although the FOR leaders listened to Farmer carefully, they were not entirely approving of his methods. Some council members asserted that defying a racist landlord, pressuring the management of a segregated coffee shop, and getting the staff of a whites-only roller skating rink arrested did not speak of love and pacifism. In the end, the National Council voted against letting Farmer form a new, national organization; instead, it gave him permission to work only with a group "along the lines he envisions in one city, Chicago," while continuing to receive his salary from the FOR.

When he returned from Columbus, Farmer met with seven of his closest associates—Bob Chino, Bernice Fisher, Joe Guinn, George Houser, Homer Jack, Jimmy Robinson, and Hugo Victoreen—to plan this new committee. They agreed to call it CORE, because it would be the very center of nonviolent direct action for an integrated society. Then they gave another meaning to the acronym: the Committee of Racial Equality. Farmer was elected the leader of this small band.

It did not take long for these dedicated activists to win CORE a reputation in Chicago. Whenever Farmer spoke publicly about the FOR, he also discussed CORE. His co-workers followed suit, as did FOR field secretary Bayard Rustin, who was not a CORE member but who nevertheless emphasized its message of nonviolence. CORE's campaign to integrate Chicago gained added momentum from the

Residents of Friendship House, an interracial Roman Catholic project in Chicago, gather for a group portrait in the early 1940s. Inspired by CORE, young people across the northern and eastern United States banded together to fight racism during these years.

white college students who joined its ranks; the product of middle-class homes, these young people were as committed to the method of nonviolent protest as they were to the goal of racial equality. With Farmer acting as the chief orchestrator, CORE moved from restaurant to restaurant, demanding service for black and white customers alike. The group also conducted stand-ins at white cafeterias and wade-ins at white beaches.

At Stoner's, a large whites-only restaurant in downtown Chicago, the management tried everything—from spilling hot food over a CORE member's head to serving CORE diners sandwiches made from garbage to kicking CORE worker George Houser in the shins—to get rid of the activists. But CORE did not relent; Stoner's did, eventually lifting its ban against black customers. Hard-fought victories such as this one prompted a Chicago National Urban League official to observe, "The Urban League is the State Department of civil rights; the NAACP is the War Department; and CORE is the marines."

News of the daring Chicago integrationists sparked interest elsewhere in the northern United States and in the West. Many FOR members in other cities were eager to start their own CORE chapters, and by the group's first anniversary several chapters had been founded. The time had come to establish a national organization that would unite all the local chapters, in spite of the FOR's opposition to such a move.

On June 15, 1943, at the Woodlawn African Methodist Episcopal Church in Chicago, Farmer presided over the first national CORE conference. Elected national chairman of the organization, Farmer helped write its charter, which called for "interracial, non-violent direct action." The CORE charter specifically stated that racism was not a "Negro problem" to be addressed only by blacks; it was every person's concern and could be erased only through the efforts of blacks and whites working together. "The stronger black nationalism becomes in Negro life in America, the farther we are from a real solution to the problem of color," said Farmer. "We cannot destroy segregation with a weapon of segregation."

Farmer thrived along with his newborn organization. During CORE's second year, chapters sprouted in New York, Philadelphia, Pittsburgh, Los Angeles, Detroit, and Seattle, greatly widening his sphere of influence. In 1942, he had chaired a handful of students at Saturday afternoon meetings; two years later, he was the leader of a growing national movement.

CORE was not alone in using nonviolence to combat Jim Crow. Also practicing Gandhian tactics was labor leader A. Philip Randolph, the guiding light behind America's largest nonviolent black protest movement, the March on Washington Movement (MOWM). During the summer of 1942, Randolph organized a series of massive rallies in Chicago, New York, and St. Louis that drew tens of thousands of people. On a smaller scale, students at Farmer's alma mater, Howard University, staged a series of sit-ins at segregated Washington, D.C., restaurants in 1943. The following year, students at Savannah State College in Georgia demonstrated against segregated buses.

But CORE's commitment to being *of* racial equality, not just *for* it, by insisting that black and white volunteers join in the struggle for civil rights, was unique. Farmer joined Randolph's March on Washington Movement, but he spoke out against the "racial chauvinism" of this all-black crusade. Indeed, CORE's interracial approach to nonviolent action would be the one adopted by the massive civil rights movement of the 1960s.

New York City policemen arrest a suspected looter during the riot that swept Harlem in August 1943. Some black leaders blamed such racial disturbances on the activities of Farmer and other "radicals"; civil rights, these conservatives asserted, should be pursued in the courts, not in the streets.

Yet there were limits to what CORE could accomplish while the nation focused its attention on World War II and its aftermath. The *Chicago Tribune* occasionally printed a short, back-page paragraph about CORE, reporting that half a dozen "screwballs" tried to get served at a segregated restaurant, but for the most part, the white media ignored the sit-ins and protests. Even the *Chicago Defender*, the city's leading black newspaper, treated CORE's activities as bizarre.

A number of influential black Americans, too, failed to see the wisdom behind importing Gandhi's nonviolent revolution to their own country. A series of race riots that erupted in 1943 made these black leaders wary of the kind of "radical" protest that Farmer encouraged. Fearing that a massive nonviolent movement would both lead to violence and diminish liberal white support, these leaders continued to believe that legislatures and courtrooms—not restaurants and street corners—were the safest places to stand up for civil rights.

Even with these hurdles to overcome, things were going well for CORE and its charismatic chairman in 1943. From the perspective of A. J. Muste, the director of the FOR, they were going perhaps too well. Muste, who had opposed Farmer's plans to make CORE into an independent national organization, now wanted to keep CORE—and Farmer—well within his grasp. Late in the year, Muste offered to double Farmer's salary and transfer him to the FOR's national office in New York City.

Farmer saw through the FOR director's reasons for handing out the promotion: In New York, Farmer would have less time for CORE, and Muste could watch over him more closely. Still, the 23-year-old Farmer greeted the transfer with enthusiasm. Ever since he had been captivated by Professor Tolson's poetry about Harlem, he had wanted to go there. "I thought that anyone who would cut wide, new swaths in the forest of American bigotry must hone his axe on the pavements of New York," Farmer said. Now he had his chance. ❧

6

"I'M NOT A QUITTER"

Although Farmer (seen here in 1958) had neither wealth nor fame when he moved to New York City in 1943, he had something even better: ideals worth dying for and the woman he loved. After trying to end her tumultuous romance with Farmer, Winnie Christie had given up and promised to marry him. "Jim, I tried to stay away," she said, "but I couldn't."

JAMES FARMER ARRIVED in New York City in late 1943, buoyed by his love for Winnie Christie, who had recently agreed to marry him, and the civil rights movement he was about to lead. But as he settled in the uptown district of Harlem, he encountered a world that was starkly different from the one in the romantic visions he had treasured since college. The cradle of much of black America's greatest cultural and intellectual achievements, Harlem struck Farmer as a far cry from "the Alice in Wonderland place of my dreams." The nation's largest black community appeared to be filled with pain and poverty rather than hope and life.

Farmer's immediate disappointment was an omen of things to come. Rather than rent an apartment, he chose to lodge in a religious retreat, a dark and dingy dwelling occupied by a former missionary to India and his followers, who had taken a vow of poverty to identify more closely with the Harlemites they sought to help. Farmer was pleased that the other residents of this retreat, or *ashram*, were disciples of Gandhi's and oriented toward nonviolent action for social change. But he had another reason for choosing to accept room and board in such squalid surroundings: It was all he could afford, even with his modest raise.

Farmer may have been making more money than he had earned in Chicago, but he enjoyed the work a lot less. His heart was with CORE, even though it did not pay him any salary. Moreover, he felt that A. J. Muste was deliberately making him miserable, sending him on endless trips to dull and remote places to keep him busy and away from CORE activities.

When Farmer was in town, the local chapter of CORE met on Friday evenings in the living room of the Harlem ashram. These meetings were among the few times Farmer felt the dreariness in his life disappear and experienced the excitement of his first days in Chicago. Using the tactics of nonviolent direct action pioneered by the Chicago chapter, the New York members of CORE zealously launched campaigns to integrate housing, barbershops, and an amusement park in the area. They picketed banks, department stores, and airlines at the same time that they negotiated for fairer hiring practices. "I still had the sensation that we were a flea gnawing on the ear of an elephant," Farmer recalled. Nevertheless, he and the other chapter members succeeded in opening up a number of jobs for blacks.

CORE was gaining in other ways as well. At the second annual convention, held in Detroit, the membership approved a change in name, from the *Committee* of Racial Equality to the *Congress* of Racial Equality, to reflect the organization's increasing size. But by evolving rapidly from an intimate gathering of friends into an organization that attracted people from all over the northern and western United States, CORE was beginning to experience growth pains.

In opening its doors to the public, CORE faced the problem of admitting unwanted guests. Many CORE members, including Farmer, especially wanted to keep out those Communists who supported the political aims of Soviet Union dictator Joseph Stalin.

By the mid-1940s, Communists in the United States had entered other organizations and allegedly re-shaped their agenda. Farmer, who was reelected national chairman at the 1944 convention, refused to let that happen to CORE. Unless the organization kept the Communists out, he warned the others, CORE might be taken over by people who were more interested in overthrowing capitalism than in fighting racial discrimination.

Some CORE members objected strongly; they believed that banning people from the organization would violate CORE's sacred ideal of personal free-dom. Farmer refused to give in. Communists would be admitted to the movement, he said, "over my dead body." CORE subsequently added to its charter a provision that excluded anyone who was loyal to a foreign government and opposed CORE's goals.

After the 1944 CORE convention, Farmer's com-mitment to the FOR continued to decline, and so did his standing with A. J. Muste. The following spring, Muste complained to Farmer that he was not orga-nizing effectively for the FOR and was not bringing in new members. Realizing that Muste wanted him to resign, Farmer made one last speaking tour through the South, then left the organization.

Farmer did not know exactly how he was going to make a living. He had no job prospects and just $850 to his name. His spirits were lifted only by the prospect of his upcoming marriage to Winnie Christie. The wedding took place in Washington, D.C., in 1945; the ceremony was performed by the Reverend J. Leonard Farmer.

A short time later, James Farmer landed a job as an organizer with the Upholsterers' International Union of North America (UIU), which represented furniture-industry workers in Virginia and North Carolina. Union organizing was a step away from race relations, but it was close enough to be enticing:

Farmer knew that in the upholstery trade, whites held the skilled jobs, whereas blacks were allowed to perform only the most menial tasks as "upholsterers' helpers." Being a union organizer put him in a position to help protect the rights of the black workers.

Stationing his wife, who was expecting their first child, with his parents in Washington, D.C., Farmer headed for Martinsville, Virginia. His first assignment was to win the allegiance of the laborers at the American Furniture Company. He positioned himself at the factory gates every dawn when the employees went to work and at midday during their lunch hour, speaking to them and handing out leaflets. In the evening, he visited the employees at home. He worked hard, but he met with little success. Few of the blacks believed that the UIU's governing body, the American Federation of Labor, was interested in fighting for black rights.

In nearby Stanleytown, Farmer fared somewhat better. Employees of the Stanley Furniture Company lived in company-owned houses and shopped at company-owned stores. "That tied them to the jobs as effectively as if they had balls and chains around their ankles," said Farmer. In a 2-week span, he managed to persuade 81 employees to join the UIU.

Triumph turned abruptly to defeat, however. The Stanley Furniture Company retaliated against the union, firing and evicting from their homes all but three of the workers who had joined. The UIU immediately filed a complaint with the National Labor Relations Board, but to no avail. "In the union wars in Virginia," Farmer noted, "fighting as hard as we might, we suffered defeat after defeat."

For Farmer, no loss was greater than the one he learned about on the day of the mass firings. When he returned to his hotel room that afternoon, he found a telegram from his sister: COME HOME AT ONCE. WINNIE MISCARRIED. NOW IN SERIOUS CONDITION AT FREED-

The original Freedom Riders—a group of CORE members who tested bus companies' compliance with desegregation rulings in 1947—prepare to embark on their Journey of Reconciliation. Farmer, who could not afford to leave his job at the time, deeply regretted his inability to join the action; it resulted in the arrest and jailing of several volunteers, including FOR field secretary Bayard Rustin (fourth from right).

MEN'S HOSPITAL. He rushed to Washington, arriving at the hospital in time to find his wife in critical condition with a high fever.

The fever finally broke, and Winnie Farmer was able to leave the hospital two weeks later. But by then, the damage to the couple's six-month-old marriage was complete. The bitterness caused by a stormy courtship and extended absences from each other was compounded by the loss of their child. Winnie moved to Chicago to live with her older sister and was granted a divorce from James in 1946.

Farmer longed to return to the fight for equal rights, but because he had to earn a living he continued his organizing work for the UIU. As a result, he missed the chance to participate in the Journey of Reconciliation, CORE's grandest effort since its founding.

In June 1946, the U.S. Supreme Court had ruled that segregated seating on buses traveling across state lines was unconstitutional. Ten months later, however, bus companies in the South were still requiring black passengers to ride in the rear. So, on April 9, 1947, 16 CORE volunteers, 8 blacks and 8 whites, boarded buses in the upper South to determine whether the Supreme Court's ruling was being upheld. The white volunteers sat in the back, and the blacks sat in front.

Sadly, the test did not turn out as CORE members had hoped it would. In North Carolina, several of the CORE workers, including Bayard Rustin, were arrested and sentenced to 30 days on a chain gang. "I felt pangs of guilt for not having been there," Farmer recalled.

He would soon feel even worse. At the end of the year, the UIU's drive in the South came to an end, and so did his employment. Without a job, without a wife, and a stranger to CORE, he headed dejectedly back to Harlem.

On his return to Harlem, however, Farmer's prospects brightened considerably. At a friend's dinner party, he became reacquainted with Lula Peterson, a white CORE worker he had met a few years earlier. She had settled in New York with the hope of

Farmer joins his second wife, the former Lula Peterson, shortly after their 1949 wedding. When doctors revealed that Peterson had cancer, she suggested canceling the wedding, but Farmer adamantly refused. "I'm not a quitter and neither are you," he told Peterson. "We're going to fight this thing through together."

becoming an actress. The two found themselves strongly attracted to each other, and, as Farmer later put it, "Before long, the inevitable came to pass." He and Peterson lived together for two years, and in March 1949 they decided to marry.

Shortly before their May wedding, the couple learned that Peterson had Hodgkin's disease, an often fatal cancer of the lymph nodes. Peterson offered Farmer a chance to bow out of the marriage. "What kind of nonsense is this?" he replied. "Of course we're going to get married. I'm not a quitter, and neither are you. We're going to fight this thing through together and lick it." And they did. Peterson, Farmer noted in his autobiography, became "the mainstay of my life for nearly three decades."

Indeed, their fortunes turned sharply for the better after they were married. The Institute of International Education, a foundation that administered international student exchange programs, offered Lula Farmer a job as its budget director; James Farmer became student field secretary of the League for Industrial Democracy (LID), an organization that promoted socialism in the United States. For the next five years, he toured college campuses and recruited young idealists for the LID.

In 1955, Farmer left the LID to take a union-organizing job with the New York City section of the American Federation of State, County, and Municipal Employees. Once again using his skills as a tactician, Farmer led workers in a huge—and ultimately successful—strike against the city's Parks Department. Farmer then directed another battle against a rival union, this time organizing poorly paid minority workers in city hospitals.

Meanwhile, Farmer and his wife helped CORE struggle along, holding meetings in their Greenwich Village apartment and participating in other local CORE activities when their schedule permitted. Lula Farmer was especially active, taking on the role of

Deputy Sheriff D. H. Lackey fingerprints Rosa Parks, the Montgomery, Alabama, seamstress who made history by refusing to move to the back of a city bus in 1955. Parks's courageous defiance of segregation law triggered a Montgomery bus boycott, which eventually brought integration to the city's transportation system.

treasurer. Keeping the national organization going was James Farmer's longtime friend Jimmy Robinson, who had taken over as executive secretary at the start of the decade. Robinson had become so adept at raising funds that by mid-1955, CORE's income exceeded its expenditures for the first time in its 13-year history.

Just when CORE was finally holding its own, a new civil rights organization was in the process of being born. Farmer came home from work on a Friday in December 1955 and heard the news on the radio that Rosa Parks, a black woman in Montgomery, Alabama, had been arrested the previous evening because she had refused to give up her bus seat to a white passenger. Within a matter of days, the eloquent and forceful minister of the Dexter Avenue Baptist Church, the Reverend Martin Luther King, Jr., helped organize a boycott of Montgomery's buses to protest the city's policy of racial discrimination. The massive boycott quickly became national news.

The following November, the U.S. Supreme Court ruled that the Alabama laws requiring segregation on buses were unconstitutional. With this victory, King—who was, like Farmer, devoted to Gandhian nonviolence and racial equality—emerged as the civil rights movement's most influential leader. In August 1957, he established the Southern Christian Leadership Conference (SCLC) to spread the principles of the Montgomery boycott and further coordinate civil rights activities in the South.

As the events unfolded, Lula Farmer seemed to read her husband's mind. He was thrilled that his dream was becoming a reality, but he was bitterly disappointed to be watching it from afar rather than making it happen. "The nonviolent movement now has the nation's attention, and it's off and running," Lula told him. "But you tilled the field, Jim. I know you'll share in the harvest. I *know* you will."

She was right. As the civil rights movement continued to blossom in the late 1950s, CORE grew along with it. "No longer did we have to explain nonviolence to people," Farmer recalled. "Thanks to Martin Luther King, it was a household word." Farmer received his share of the credit. Throughout the movement, people acknowledged him as one of the nation's leading authorities on nonviolent protest. Only in his late thirties, he had nevertheless gained the status of elder statesman.

A busload of Texas women share a triumphant moment in April 1956, shortly after the Supreme Court's ruling that segregation of public transportation within a state was unconstitutional. Like most other civil rights victories, this one was the result of the direct, nonviolent methods espoused by Farmer, the Reverend Martin Luther King, Jr., and others.

Four freshmen from North Carolina Agricultural & Technical State University—(left to right) David Richmond, Franklin McCain, Ezell Blair, Jr., and Joseph McNeill—leave the Greensboro variety store where they had spent the day patiently waiting for service at the whites-only lunch counter. This peaceful sit-in, duplicated across the South, finally resulted in the desegregation of lunch counters in more than 200 communities.

On Valentine's Day in February 1959, Farmer took on another role—that of father—with the birth of his and his wife's first child: Tami Lynn, a healthy, strong girl with a sandy complexion and a heart-shaped face. It seemed that each time Farmer's private life flowered, so did his public life. In early 1959, he regained a central position in the civil rights struggle he had helped nurture since its infancy. Roy Wilkins, the head of the NAACP, hired him to be program director, a post in which he was to devise new activities in the fight for black rights.

"What I proposed," Farmer said, "was that we identify the problem areas affecting black Americans, define the objectives in each area, designate the methods likely to be most effective in each, and indicate who should do it and establish a timetable. In short, for each problem, there should be answers to the questions: what, how, who, where, and when." Interoffice politics interceded, however, and the NAACP failed to act on his proposal. Instead, Farmer spent his time speaking at rallies and fund-raising dinners—decidedly not the duties he had been hired to perform.

Meanwhile, nonviolent demonstrations snowballed across the South. The protests intensified on February 1, 1960, when four black university students in Greensboro, North Carolina, sat down at a whites-only lunch counter and waited patiently to be served. The North Carolina Agricultural & Technical State University freshmen remained there until the store closed, then returned the next morning with 19 of their friends. The following day, the students, whose number had swelled to 85, sat in shifts of several hours each.

The lunch-counter sit-in, which was much like the nonviolent protests Farmer and his friends had staged 20 years earlier, galvanized a national movement, the Student Non-Violent Coordinating Committee (SNCC). Sit-ins against segregation sprang up in other cities, capturing the attention of the national media and attracting increasing waves of new student volunteers. The demonstrations worked: By the end of 1961, store owners in 200 southern cities had desegregated their lunch counters.

This was a pivotal year for Farmer as well. Ready to accept its share of the burden in expanding the nonviolent protest movement, CORE, which now boasted more than 40 chapters across the nation, began to look for a bolder, more charismatic leader and public speaker than the bureaucratic whiz Jimmy Robinson. CORE's National Action Council created a new position, national director, and considered two men for the job: Martin Luther King, Jr., and James Farmer.

King was offered the post first, but when he declined it to remain with the SCLC, CORE turned to its founder. Farmer resigned from the NAACP, and on February 1, 1961—exactly one year after the first sit-in at the F.W. Woolworth lunch counter in Greensboro—he became CORE's first national director. After nearly two decades of wandering in the woods, James Farmer had found his way home. ❧

7

THE FREEDOM RIDES

W HEN JAMES FARMER told Roy Wilkins in early 1961 that he was leaving the NAACP to head CORE, Wilkins smiled, like a man who wished that he, too, was on his way to the front lines. "You're going to be riding a mustang pony," Wilkins said, "while I'm riding a dinosaur."

Farmer wasted no time in mounting his steed. On February 1, his first day as national director of CORE, he huddled with his closest aides—Gordon Carey, Jim McCain, Marvin Rich, and Jimmy Robinson—in CORE's New York City office. The five men focused on the hundreds of college students who had launched new protests against Jim Crow to commemorate the first anniversary of the Greensboro, North Carolina, sit-in.

Of all the demonstrations, the one in Rock Hill, South Carolina, drew the most attention. On the morning of January 31, CORE field secretary Thomas Gaither and nine Friendship Junior College students had staged a sit-in at McCrory's, a department store with a segregated lunch counter. Promptly arrested, the students were soon convicted of trespassing, and they were sentenced to pay a $100 fine or spend 30 days on a road gang. They chose to go to jail.

After deliberately using the "wrong"—blacks-only—waiting room, three white Freedom Riders head for jail in Jackson, Mississippi, on June 2, 1961. Following in Farmer's footsteps, the trio had arrived in the southern city one week after the CORE leader's arrest.

Dazed Freedom Riders watch helplessly as their bus, torched by a white mob in May 1961, burns to the ground near Anniston, Alabama. A companion bus escaped the mob on the road, but at the Anniston bus station, its unarmed passengers were attacked by a gang of local thugs wielding lengths of iron pipe. "If any man says that he had no fear in the action of the sixties," said Farmer, "he is a liar."

Their jail-in received national attention, as Gaither and the others had hoped, and their protest grew when four SNCC leaders raced to Rock Hill to capitalize on the publicity. Following in the footsteps of the CORE demonstrators, the SNCC leaders got themselves arrested, refused to pay their fines, and went to jail. For the first time in the civil rights movement, demonstrators had traveled outside their own community to take part in a protest.

CORE's national director recognized the tremendous potential of this new tactic. The surest way to defeat Jim Crow was for the separate units of the civil rights movement to combine their forces instead of relying on isolated boycotts. Farmer also urged activists to fill up the jails, thereby creating a problem that the government would have to address. Gandhi, he remembered, had successfully employed this strategy in India.

After examining their options carefully, Farmer and his aides decided to reenact the 1947 Journey of Reconciliation, but with several new twists. The protesters would not only ride on segregated buses but would extend their campaign of civil disobedience to bus terminals. Even though the U.S. Supreme Court had recently ruled against segregation in bus stations used in interstate travel, terminal accommodations remained segregated throughout the southern states. Accordingly, the riders would travel to the Deep South—Georgia, Mississippi, Louisiana, and Alabama—where Jim Crow was most powerful.

"We were counting on the bigots in the South to do our work for us," Farmer said later. "We figured that the government would have to respond if we created a situation that was headline news all over the world."

After three months of planning, seven blacks and six whites boarded two buses in Washington, D.C., on May 4, thus beginning the journey that Farmer dubbed the Freedom Ride. At age 41, he was the oldest black in the group. Among the others who rode with him were 2 CORE staffers and 21-year-old John Lewis, a member of the SCLC and soon to be the SNCC's national chairman. Each volunteer had attended two weeks of training sessions to prepare for any eventuality, including being physically assaulted.

In the bus terminal in Fredericksburg, Virginia, just 50 miles south of the nation's capital, the Freedom Riders saw the first indications of segregation: signs that said White and Colored. They would soon see more. As the buses traveled through North Carolina and crept into South Carolina, "we began to taste southern hate," Farmer recalled. For the most part, though, the trip was failing to generate the kind of publicity CORE wanted. The first 10 days of

the campaign went smoothly, with the riders enjoy-
ing the applause of large crowds of supporters in the
black communities where they stopped each night.

Back in Washington, D.C., Farmer's parents
followed the Freedom Ride with interest and appre-
hension. J. Leonard was in Freedmen's Hospital,
dying of cancer, and his fears about what might
happen to his son compounded his suffering. The
elder Farmer knew the South well enough to understand that the Freedom Riders might be safe all the
way through Georgia but that once they crossed the
border into Alabama, they would be in mortal
danger. Each day, he checked the riders' itinerary;
and on May 13, soon after he saw that the next day
would take them into Alabama, he died. His wife
later said that he had timed his death to interrupt
their son's trip before he could reach the most
dangerous part of the Freedom Ride.

Farmer abruptly left the protest to fly home for his
father's funeral. Word reached him later in the day
that a furious white mob had firebombed one of the
buses several miles outside Anniston, Alabama. A
photographer on the scene managed to get a shot of
the passengers fleeing from the flame-engulfed bus as
it burned to the ground, thus capturing for the entire
nation the fury of racial hatred in the South.

The police, arriving conspicuously late, whisked
the riders to a local hospital, where they were treated
for smoke inhalation. Fortunately, all the passengers
had managed to escape from the burning bus without
suffering any serious injuries. The riders on the other
bus were not as fortunate. Eight white thugs boarded
the motor coach at the Anniston station and began
savagely beating its passengers. One of them, Dr.
Walter Bergman, suffered permanent brain damage.

Fred Shuttlesworth, head of Birmingham's SCLC
chapter, arranged for the first group of riders to be
conveyed safely to his Alabama city. Again, the

Weary activists in the Reverend Ralph Abernathy's Montgomery, Alabama, church wait out a night of terror in the eventful month of May 1961. Outside, only the presence of federal marshals kept a screaming mob from burning down the packed church.

protesters on the second bus were not as lucky. They were attacked for a second time as their bus pulled into the Birmingham terminal. "It looks like there has been a hog killing on this bus!" exclaimed a bystander.

Bloodied and overwhelmed by the violent reaction to their nonviolent protest, the Freedom Riders called off the rest of their planned journey and escaped from Birmingham on a special flight arranged by the U.S. Justice Department. The following day, however, two of the original riders, John Lewis and Henry Thomas, set out with eight SNCC youths to resume the Freedom Ride to Montgomery, Alabama. Farmer arranged for a replacement team of CORE members to link up with the second group of riders in Montgomery. Then he headed there himself.

By the time Farmer arrived, another white mob had attacked the second group of Freedom Riders, this time at the Montgomery bus station. Martin Luther King, Jr., flew to the city, too, to show support for Montgomery's black community and to quell its anger. He immediately arranged for a rally to be held at the First Baptist Church, the ministry of his chief aide, Rev. Ralph Abernathy. More than a thousand blacks assembled to hear King speak.

A hostile white mob showed up, too, and threatened to set the church on fire. Five hundred federal marshals sent by U.S. attorney general Robert F. Kennedy tried to keep the club-wielding rioters at bay. Inside, the crowd prayed and sang hymns and waited all night for the marshals to disperse the mob.

On the following afternoon, May 23, Farmer, King, Abernathy, Lewis, and student leader Diane Nash held a press conference in Abernathy's backyard. Despite the threats, they said, the Freedom Ride would continue on to Jackson, Mississippi, as planned.

It resumed the following morning. Under a heavy guard of federal marshals, Farmer and 26 other volunteers ate breakfast at the Montgomery terminal and "readied themselves," Farmer said, "for their ride into bigotry's main den." The scene around the bus station resembled a war zone, with military jeeps patrolling the streets and government helicopters circling above. Some of the young riders scrawled the names and addresses of their closest relatives on pieces of paper and tucked them into their pocket, in case they did not make it safely to Jackson.

The two Freedom Ride buses rolled into Mississippi without incident as the protesters sang

> I'm a-takin' a ride
> On the Greyhound bus line.
> I'm a-ridin' the *front seat*
> To Jackson, this time.

When the Freedom Riders finally arrived at the Jackson bus station on May 24, they found the terminal crowded but hauntingly quiet. Looking out their windows, the activists saw rows of solemn white faces staring silently at them. Farmer linked his arms with another rider and led the way through the crowd to the whites-only waiting room, where he sipped water from the whites-only drinking fountain. Then he walked over to the whites-only restaurant. The Jackson police chief blocked the entrance.

Three times, he told Farmer to "move on." Each time, Farmer respectfully declined. The riders were then arrested for attempting to use whites-only facilities and were transported to the Jackson City Jail. Farmer later said of the incident, "It was all very civilized"; and for a good reason: "The nation was watching through newsreel cameras."

When the doors to the Jackson City Jail slammed shut, however, the polite manners and the sweet smell of magnolia blossoms gave way to the harshness of prison life. After a brief trial, all 27 of the Freedom Riders were convicted. Twenty-two of them, including Farmer, refused to pay the $200 fine and faced 67 days in jail.

Back in New York, Lula Farmer took great pride in her husband's brave stand, as did their two-year-old daughter. Whenever Tami went for a walk with her mother, she would announce to passersby, "My daddy's in *jail!*"

Meanwhile, King and other black leaders were being flooded with advice, even from strong supporters, to slow down and begin a "cooling-off period." Farmer's response to such suggestions was terse and to the point: "We had been cooling off for 100 years," he said. "If we got any cooler we'd be in a deep freeze."

CORE, the SNCC, and the SCLC promptly set up a Freedom Ride Coordinating Committee to launch more trips. "Got your bus ticket?" became a common greeting among civil rights supporters across the nation. A jail sentence, Farmer declared, "was not a punishment, but a triumph."

Farmer found little to celebrate, however, in being shuttled from the Jackson City Jail to the

Doing their best to ignore the abuse of contemptuous whites, an interracial trio of protesters doggedly keep their seats at a Jackson lunch counter. Sit-ins—originated 20 years earlier by Farmer and his colleagues—took place all over the South in the 1960s, eventually wearing down the barriers erected by Jim Crow.

Hinds County Jail to the Hinds County Prison Farm. On his first morning at the prison farm, he overheard an inmate being beaten with blackjacks for refusing to call his keepers Sir. Fortunately for Farmer, another rider was bailed out that same day and immediately held a press conference. The rider's account of the beating prompted the authorities to return Farmer to the Hinds County Jail before any harm could come to him.

He did not stay there for long, though. As more and more protesters began to fill the Jackson jails, Farmer was transferred to the Parchman State Prison, where he was placed in a 6-by-9-foot cell. He was allowed to shower twice a week, but he was permitted practically no other comforts: no television, no exercise, and no reading material other than two letters a week.

The prison officials did almost everything they could to humble Farmer and his fellow activists, including overcrowding their cells. Nevertheless, the CORE leader refused to call a halt to the swelling protest, which was generating considerable attention. The news media's coverage, especially of the first two Freedom Rides, had seen to that.

Farmer soon discovered he had become a hero to thousands of civil rights supporters. Flying directly to New York after his July release from the Parchman State Prison, he stepped off the plane to find himself staring into a battery of flashbulbs, television cameras, and microphones, as an enthusiastic crowd shouted, "We shall overcome!" and "Farmer is our leader!" WELCOME HOME, BIG JIM, read a giant banner. Farmer hugged his daughter and his wife, who was six months pregnant with their second child, Abbey Lee, and received a warm greeting from his CORE staff.

During Farmer's absence, CORE had drawn on his sudden celebrity to recruit backers and volunteers by the hundreds. The organization had then spent more than $100,000 in arranging for smaller Freedom Rides to spread the gospel of nonviolence throughout the South. The protesters traveled from Washington, D.C., to Florida, from Missouri to Louisiana, and from Virginia to Arkansas, and they filled up the jails everywhere they went, especially in Jackson.

By the time Farmer resumed his role as national director in July, CORE had established itself as a major force in the black protest movement. ❧

8

"WE HAVEN'T GONE
FAR ENOUGH"

Convicted of disturbing the peace
after leading a 1963 civil rights
protest in Plaquemine, Louisiana,
Farmer gestures toward City
Hall, where he had just heard his
sentence pronounced. Although he
could have paid a $300 fine and
gone free, the CORE leader chose
to join his fellow demonstrators in
jail.

THE SUMMER OF 1961 proved to be a resounding success for James Farmer and CORE. The federal government, under more pressure than ever to take action against Jim Crow facilities, ordered that legislation banning segregated bus stations be enforced. Train companies also were told to abandon their Jim Crow sections, as were most airports.

By February 1962, a year after he had assumed leadership of CORE, Farmer believed that Jim Crow in interstate transportation was nearly dead. The lesson seemed clear. "When the heat is on," he said, change comes swiftly. "We have to continue to create crises like the Freedom Rides." Under his direction, CORE did just that.

As in the past, Farmer strove to be a true leader instead of an armchair general who dispatches his troops to the battlefield and then remains comfortably behind the front lines. He was in the driver's seat both in spirit and in person when CORE began its Freedom Highways campaign in August 1962. Seeking to make the roadways free of segregated facilities, he led more than 1,000 demonstrators in a sit-in at one of the many Howard Johnson's restaurants along Route 40 in Durham, North Carolina. Before long, other waves of protesters were holding sit-ins along the highway, and they did not stop until half of their targets had been desegregated.

But working to integrate public accommodations was only one of Farmer's goals. Growing more ambitious every day, CORE broadened its objectives not just in the South but on all points of the compass. Chapters in Los Angeles and Newark organized sit-ins to open up better housing; Seattle and Denver CORE units successfully picketed grocery chains for more jobs; the Philadelphia branch began to fight discrimination in trade unions. CORE workers stationed themselves in front of trucks and bulldozers, chained themselves to doorways, and clogged up roadways in an effort to achieve their demands.

CORE staged three of its most dramatic demonstrations in the North Carolina cities of Durham, Greensboro, and High Point. Rather than focus on isolated cases of racial injustice, CORE attempted to achieve something much more spectacular. Unleashing their three-pronged attack in March 1963, Farmer and his staff demanded the complete desegregation of *all* public facilities.

The North Carolina campaign reached its height in mid-May, when nearly 1,000 protesters in Greensboro (including North Carolina A&T University student body president Jesse Jackson) were arrested within a three-day span. Like the general that he was, Farmer immediately rallied his Greensboro troops, telling 1,200 supporters on May 19 that they were fighting a "second Revolutionary War." "This drive for freedom is spreading all over the country," he added. "There can be no stopping now." That night in Durham, 700 more demonstrators were arrested for holding a sit-in.

The next day, Terry Sanford, the governor of North Carolina, angrily accused CORE of going too far in encouraging young people to get arrested. "I'm serving notice that we haven't gone far enough," an equally incensed Farmer said, and he vowed that more arrests would follow. The marches, boycotts,

sit-ins, and protest rallies continued, until the three cities agreed to establish biracial commissions to work toward integration. Only then did CORE declare a truce.

CORE did not take a militant stance in all its campaigns. Bowing to the argument that the best way for black Americans to achieve equality was through the ballot box, many civil rights activists, including Farmer's former NAACP boss Roy Wilkins, spearheaded a move to register black voters in the South. Farmer enlisted CORE's membership in the voter registration drive.

A patrolman and his German shepherd attack a black bystander during a May 1963 civil rights demonstration in Birmingham, Alabama. Looking at photographs such as this one, President John F. Kennedy said, "I can well understand why the Negroes of Birmingham are tired of being asked to be patient."

Bayard Rustin, chief organizer of the March on Washington, pauses outside his Manhattan headquarters in August 1963. An assistant to Martin Luther King, Rustin specialized in planning and directing demonstrations; his most spectacular production was the 1963 march, which produced King's unforgettable "I Have a Dream" speech. Originally part of the program, Farmer wound up watching it on television from a Louisiana prison.

Farmer remained committed, however, to capitalizing on CORE's recent momentum. Using the Gandhian tactics of negotiation, protest, and peaceful disobedience, he continued to direct CORE workers to conduct boycotts and sit-ins against companies that discriminated against blacks. In most of these cases, CORE succeeded at the negotiation stage, thereby averting a public demonstration. When Farmer wrote to the Sears Roebuck department store chain, for example, and demanded to know why the company had so few high-level black employees, Sears promptly made room for 25 upper-management blacks. On those occasions when negotiations failed, CORE would hold a demonstration; wearying of the negative publicity, the beleaguered company often gave in to CORE's demands.

On June 19, 1963, in an attempt to coordinate the activities of the major civil rights organizations more effectively, millionaire philanthropist Stephen Currier hosted a breakfast discussion that was attended by the so-called Big Six of black leadership: James Farmer; Martin Luther King, Jr.; John Lewis; Roy Wilkins; National Coucil of Negro Women president Dorothy Height; and National Urban League executive secretary Whitney Young. They discussed the possibility of joint fund-raising and other programs that might draw their competing organizations together. They decided to call themselves the Council on United Civil Rights Leadership and to meet periodically to hash out their differences.

Meanwhile, a much broader plan to unite the major civil rights organizations was taking shape. In early 1963, A. Philip Randolph and Bayard Rustin had begun to lay the groundwork for a massive demonstration in the nation's capital: the March on Washington for Jobs and Freedom. CORE agreed to sponsor the march, as did the NAACP, the SCLC, the SNCC, the Urban League, and many other organizations.

The conflicting politics of the participating groups, as well as the pressure put on them by President John F. Kennedy's administration, eventually led to a change in the march's main objective. Struck from the plans was any form of civil disobedience to promote black employment; a giant rally to encourage passage of a civil rights bill was scheduled instead. According to Farmer, "Our representatives wanted the march to be one of protest against the recalcitrance of bigotry and segregation, and the as yet relative inactivity of the federal government on our behalf. Others wanted it to be a testament of hope and faith and prayer."

Farmer and CORE were not alone in expressing their impatience with the pace of social change. A

Militant young San Franciscans offer a black power salute in the mid-1960s. Although Farmer sympathized with blacks who demanded swift social justice, he never abandoned his faith in what he called "direct nonviolence."

Farmer addresses a group of supporters in Boston. He usually preached nonviolence, but acts of mindless savagery could drive even this moderate man to extremes. "I was not Christ," he said after a band of whites murdered three young CORE workers in Mississippi. "I was not Gandhi. I was not King. I wanted to kill those men—not with bullets, but with my fingers around their throats."

growing number of black activists, especially the younger militants, were no longer satisfied with token gains. Black nationalist leader Malcolm X expressed his willingness to condone violence in the fight against Jim Crow and called the planned march "the Farce on Washington." Many other young blacks echoed his angry defiance, including former Freedom Rider Stokely Carmichael. "Freedom Now!" became their battle cry.

Responding to this new brand of black militance, Farmer published several articles in June 1963 in which he said he would try to channel the rising anger among black Americans into nonviolent rather than violent action. Still, he warned, the cities were ready to explode with anger. "It will be a long, hot summer," he predicted.

It had already been a tumultuous spring. In early May, police in Birmingham, Alabama, had un-leashed their attack dogs on crowds of civil rights demonstrators; fire fighters had employed high-pressure water hoses to repel the protesters. President Kennedy, viewing the events on the television news broadcasts, said that the pictures had made him "sick."

He was not alone. Horrified by what had taken place in Birmingham, young activists hurried to CORE and other civil rights organizations to take part in the protests; nonviolent demonstrations began to engulf the nation. When Mississippi NAACP leader Medgar Evers was assassinated outside his Jackson home in mid-June, the tide of direct action rose even higher.

Farmer, who was scheduled to be one of the featured speakers at the March on Washington rally, visited the White House on June 22, accompanied by King, Lewis, Randolph, Wilkins, Young, and a few others. President Kennedy, fearing an outbreak of violence during the march, had summoned the black leaders to suggest that they cancel it. "If we called the street demonstrations off and then were defeated in the legislative battle," Farmer told him, "the result would be that frustration would grow into violence." The march remained set for August 28.

In the meantime, Farmer kept busy. Nine days prior to the march, he led 500 civil rights activists through the streets of Plaquemine, Louisiana, to dramatize the plight of its black community, which received hardly any public services. Not surprisingly, the rally received little sympathy from the city authorities. Mounted on horseback, the local police used tear gas, billy clubs, and electric cattle prods to subdue and arrest more than 200 of the demonstrators, including Farmer.

With the March on Washington only a few days away, Wilkins and Young urged Farmer to bail himself out of jail. Farmer refused to leave his fellow protesters. "I cannot come out of jail while they are still in," he wired back to the civil rights leaders, "for their crime was the same as mine—demanding freedom now." Instead, he watched the massive rally on the television set that his supporters had brought to his jail cell. The spectacle of more than a quarter of a million people—blacks and whites—marching through the nation's capital in a show of brotherhood prompted him to weep with joy.

A resolute Farmer wasted little time in returning to action after the Plaquemine police chief released him from jail on August 31. The following day, Farmer regrouped his forces at the Plymouth Rock Baptist Church for a march that snaked its way through the city's streets. Their final destination was the police chief's home.

In the middle of the demonstration—just when Farmer's troops had reached Plaquemine's main square—hordes of mounted police surrounded the marchers and urged them to abandon their campaign. When the protesters refused to leave, the police converged on the crowd and used their billy clubs

Grimacing in pain, a demonstrator flees state policemen in Plaquemine on August 21, 1963. Farmer, who had led a 500-person protest march through the town, recalled the day's events with horror. "The mounted troopers with their prod rods," he said, "rode down the marchers like cowboys on a fearsome roundup."

and electric prods to shut down the rally. "I watched the Negroes coming back," Farmer remembered, "those who could run, bleeding, hysterical, faint, some of the stronger ones carrying the injured."

After taping over their nameplates and badge numbers to shield their identity, the police continued their assault. First, they employed tear gas to drive the marchers back to their starting place, then they turned on high-pressure water hoses and flooded the church. Word spread quickly among the protesters that the police were searching for the organizers of the rally.

When no leaders were found in the gutted church, the police turned their attention to the parsonage behind it. Standing a safe distance away, they fired several canisters of tear gas into the building. "Almost everyone inside was blinded and choking," recalled Farmer, who was one of the many demonstrators trapped in the parsonage. "The noise of the screaming was unbearable."

Desperate for oxygen, some people writhed on the floor to escape the clouds of gas. Others attempted to run out the rear door, but the police blocked their way and forced them back inside. "We tried to telephone for help, but the operators were not putting through any outgoing calls from the Negro section," Farmer said. "We could hear the screaming on the streets as the troopers on horseback resumed their sport with the cattle prods and billy clubs." Back in New York City, Tami Farmer heard on the news that her father was in grave danger. Terrified, the little girl hid under her bed.

Farmer eventually managed to escape from the parsonage by crawling through waist-high grass under the cover of dusk. He reached a nearby funeral parlor, where hundreds of other protesters had taken refuge. Later that night, the Plaquemine police finally figured out he was hiding there and called for

Gathered in the unsafe shelter of the Plymouth Rock Baptist Church in Plaquemine, demonstrators shout defiance at besieging troopers. Louisiana lawmen, intent on finding Farmer, flooded the church soon after this photograph was taken, but the CORE chief's supporters managed to spirit him out of town in a hearse.

Arms linked, Farmer and three other CORE members block the entrance to the New York City Pavilion at the 1964 World's Fair. "We were courting arrest—even asking for it," Farmer recalled later, "in order to gain a forum for discussions with the city on the issues of [employment, housing, and educational] discrimination."

Farmer to give himself up. But before he could step forward, a few of the refugees grabbed him. "We're not going to let you go out there tonight," one man whispered. "That's a lynch mob. You go out there tonight, you won't be alive tomorrow morning."

Moments later, an officer shouted to the people inside, "We'll give you just five minutes to get Farmer out here." At that, the owner of the parlor strode up to the lawmen and demanded to see their search warrant. Unable to produce one, the officers withdrew to reshape their plans.

Knowing full well it was only a matter of time before the authorities returned for Farmer, a couple of his allies hid him in the second of two hearses housed in the parlor's garage. The first car acted as a decoy by racing out of the building and engaging the police. A few minutes later, when the streets seemed clear, the second hearse sped out of the garage. Farmer spent the next four and a half hours weaving his way across the back roads of Louisiana in the rear of the hearse. The car did not stop until he had safely reached New Orleans.

Farmer held a press conference the next day and then returned to Plaquemine to face his pursuers in broad daylight. He went directly to the local courthouse and stood on its steps, waiting to be served with a warrant for his arrest. None appeared; the last thing the Plaquemine police wanted was to be scrutinized by the media. Farmer returned to New York triumphant but hardly unscathed. The tear gas had hurt his eyes so badly that when he went blind 20 years later, he was convinced the loss of his eyesight was a result of his horrifying night in Plaquemine.

To an increasing number of civil rights activists, the Plaquemine manhunt was proof of what they had been saying all along: It makes no sense to talk about loving one's enemies if they continue to respond in the most savage way imaginable. Skip the negotiations and forget trying to change Jim Crow's heart, they said. The time has come to take what is rightfully ours.

Farmer ends his 1964 World's Fair sit-in, a far cry from his demonstration in Louisiana earlier that year. "Look out. Be very careful. Don't hurt him," said one New York City police officer. "Gee, Mr. Farmer, you got to lose some weight," remarked another. "I had to laugh," recalled the usually solemn CORE chief.

Four of the nation's most influential black leaders discuss the 1964 Civil Rights Act with President Lyndon B. Johnson at the White House. Participants in the dialogue are (left to right) NAACP executive director Roy Wilkins; Farmer; SCLC chief Martin Luther King, Jr.; Whitney Young of the National Urban League; and Johnson.

Farmer understood the more militant wing of his organization and its eagerness to turn up the intensity of the protests. He agreed that CORE would have to change its tactics if it wanted to keep pace with the opposition. "We have had our rights blocked for 100 years," he said. "It is time for all Americans to realize how it feels to have your way blocked." But Farmer was unwilling to become more militant. He still believed that nonviolent action was the best method for black Americans to gain their rights.

Meanwhile, various branches of CORE stepped up their civil disobedience campaigns. One of the most highly publicized demonstrations took place in March 1964, when several CORE members blocked traffic on New York City's Triborough Bridge during rush hour. The protesters undertook this action to draw attention to the problem of overcrowding in Harlem schools. Farmer objected to this sort of approach: Demonstrations that inconvenienced the public, he said, "were likely to achieve nothing more than irritation and the alienation of many CORE sympathizers."

Farmer also opposed a scheme that the Brooklyn chapter of CORE proposed less than a month later: To protest substandard education and housing for blacks in New York City, the group planned to obstruct all roads leading to the New York World's Fair on its opening day, April 22. Farmer asked the planners to abandon their massive stall-in. When they refused, he suspended the chapter's personnel. The Brooklyn CORE members responded by going ahead with their plans.

Faced with a challenge to his authority, Farmer met it head-on. He disapproved publicly of the stall-in and organized his own demonstration inside the fairgrounds. On the day of the planned protests, only two cars joined the stall-in. Meanwhile, nearly 300 supporters joined Farmer in his demonstration in front of the New York City Pavilion.

In spite of this display of solidarity, CORE's foundation was beginning to crack. As effective as the organization was, it was never very large; at its peak, CORE boasted about 5,000 members, most of whom were activists, not bureaucrats. Accordingly, a few problems could easily put a dent in its operations.

By the summer of 1964, CORE's troubles had clearly begun to mount. Expanding its efforts to win jobs and fair housing for blacks, especially the urban poor in the North, CORE saw its expenditures rise until its coffers became bare. Moreover, with the organization drawing closer to its goal of destroying segregation, CORE's membership divided into two camps: those who sided with Farmer's tactics of nonviolent direct action, and those who said the changing times called for more radical methods. And even Farmer's supporters agreed that he was a less than effective administrator.

The scales tipped in the militants' favor on July 2, when President Lyndon B. Johnson signed the Civil Rights Act of 1964. This act outlawed segregation in public facilities, prohibited unions and employers from practicing racial discrimination, and authorized the withholding of federal funds from institutions that continued to discriminate against blacks. In effect, the Civil Rights Act killed Jim Crow. Ironically, it also diminished the need for direct nonviolent action and thereby contributed to the declining health of CORE. ✦

9
"A CRISIS OF VICTORY"

$\mathbf{A}$S THE CIVIL rights struggle increases," James Farmer told his staff in the spring of 1964, "so has the frustration of the Negro people." Concluding that nonviolent direct action had achieved all it could, a large segment of black America had begun to advocate the use of force to attain equal rights. When this cry for militancy spilled over into CORE, Farmer sought to silence it by calling on his powers of charm and diplomacy.

Farmer had long since earned the loyalty of CORE's rank and file by participating in protests and refusing bail when he was jailed. He retained the members' affection by being his affable self and making good use of his gift for oratory. Equally at home at a street-corner rally and a banquet hall, Farmer aroused his listeners with tales of racial injustice and amused them with wry anecdotes. When he spoke of devotion to the cause of civil rights, no one questioned his motives.

But not even Farmer could shield CORE from the violent events of the so-called Freedom Summer of 1964.

Farmer joins a CORE picket line in Bogalusa, Louisiana, in 1965. This demonstration, like many others staged in both the South and the North, aimed at increasing the employment of blacks in white-owned stores that catered largely to black customers.

The summer began with Farmer receiving a phone call at 3:00 A.M. on June 22. The caller, CORE's Mississippi field secretary, George Raymond, informed him that an interracial team of young CORE workers—James Chaney, Andrew Goodman, and Michael Schwerner—had disappeared near the small Mississippi town of Philadelphia. The activists, Raymond feared, had been murdered.

Farmer arrived in Mississippi that same day to help search for the three missing men. Although the hunt was joined by the FBI, local law officers, and U.S. Navy men stationed nearby, the CORE workers' bodies were not discovered until six and a half weeks later. All had been shot to death. And even though their deaths were clearly the act of white racists, no one was ever charged with murder.

The slaying of Chaney, Goodman, and Schwerner kicked off a summer of utter savagery. In the South, black churches were firebombed. In the North, race riots erupted in New York, Chicago, and Philadelphia, among other cities.

Farmer was in his Manhattan apartment on the night of July 18 when word reached him that Harlem was exploding in violence. He hurried off at once to CORE's Harlem office, where two dozen CORE members awaited him. "It's a war," one of them told Farmer.

Earlier that evening, CORE workers had held a rally to protest the killing of James Powell, a black youth who had been fatally shot by a white policeman. The rally soon got out of hand, with some of the demonstrators throwing bricks and bottles at the police. By the time Farmer arrived on the scene, 125th Street, Harlem's main thoroughfare, was being patrolled on one side by scores of black youths and on the other side by pistol-wielding, steel-helmeted policemen.

Farmer left the CORE office to talk to the youths. He told them to clear the streets and to leave the fighting to "the great freedom movement, with King, and CORE, and SNCC, which was battering down barriers and was going to change the face of this nation." The crowd greeted him with boos.

"Now, I'm bringing that movement north," Farmer continued, "so we can deal with the problems of the northern ghettos—the rat-infested firetrap housing; the garbage piling up because no sanitation trucks come by; the unemployment, when there are jobs for whites, but not for blacks; and the *police brutality.*" Gradually, Farmer, the consummate public speaker, won the crowd over. Then, at New York NAACP president Joe Overton's suggestion, he turned the rabble into an orderly group and led it on a march through Harlem. "We want justice!" the assembly chanted as it paraded through the streets. "We want justice!" Unsure of the marchers' intentions, the police kept pace with them.

Before long, some of the youths began to throw bottles and bricks at the police, who responded with gunfire. The shots triggered another assault from the marchers that was returned by the lawmen. "They were firing at windows and rooftops," Farmer remembered, "and answering bricks with bullets on the street."

A distraught Farmer managed to make it back safely to the Harlem CORE office. There, he stared out the window, his gaze resting on the capital of black America now burning with rage. Legalized segregation may have been destroyed, but its legacy lived on.

That was true even in his own organization. CORE had always been the most integrated of any major civil rights group. Many of the blacks in CORE were now arguing, though, that whites in the organization should not be allowed to hold positions of leadership.

CORE's national director was caught in the middle of the conflict. "We are not the paragons of

Seated in the ruins of a firebombed black church in Philadelphia, Mississippi, Farmer awaits the start of a 1965 memorial service for James Chaney, Andrew Goodman, and Michael Schwerner, the young CORE workers found murdered near Philadelphia in 1964. Holding her grandchild is James Chaney's mother, Fannie Lee Chaney.

"Jim, you'd better get your ass up here fast!" said the CORE worker who called Farmer at 1:00 A.M. on July 18, 1964. "Harlem is blowing like a volcano! Bottles and bricks are flying everywhere, and the cops are shooting like cowboys." Farmer hastened to Harlem, but not even his fabled eloquence could chill the violent encounter, one of many that scarred Harlem during the early 1960s.

love that we once were, to be sure," he preached, "but we do not hate." To restore what CORE's national council referred to as the "breakdown of CORE discipline," Farmer developed a bold new plan. In October 1964, he proposed a New Directions program for CORE.

Farmer shaped this program to help blacks develop a greater voice in their own affairs. While pressing politicians to aid black communities, CORE members were to assist the black poor in starting their own businesses and in forming cooperatives to produce goods for general use. CORE chapters would also provide clothes for needy families, work to clean up black neighborhoods, start up tenants' rights groups to tackle housing issues, and establish programs to teach young people about black history and culture. A program that built up racial pride, Farmer believed, would turn blacks away from the growing black nationalist movement.

Despite Farmer's good intentions, the New Directions campaign failed to halt CORE's decline.

Even though CORE added 30 new chapters between the summer of 1964 and mid-1965—giving the organization 144 branches across the nation—it was claiming success less often. After four years of making steady headway, CORE found itself having to tackle problems, such as the concerns of the black poor, that could not be remedied solely by direct nonviolent action.

"The Civil Rights Revolution has been caught up in a crisis of victory," A. Philip Randolph acknowledged in his opening remarks at the 1965 Conference of Negro Leaders, "a crisis which may involve great opportunity or great danger to its future fulfillment." For Farmer and CORE, it was the latter.

The civil rights movement enjoyed some bright spots in late 1964 and into 1965: the gearing up of the War on Poverty, President Lyndon B. Johnson's attempt to channel federal funds to the poor, and the passage of the Voting Rights Act of 1965. For the most part, though, the civil rights campaigns that CORE carried out, such as the protests Farmer attended in Bogalusa, Louisiana, followed a typical pattern: Demonstrations were held, the authorities agreed to meet the protesters' demands, and then the politicians broke their promises.

The national literacy program that Farmer attempted to get off the ground in late 1964 met a similar fate. That October, after an encouraging meeting with President Johnson, he sent to the White House a detailed plan to train thousands of CORE and SNCC activists as reading instructors. To be initiated in 10 major cities before it expanded nationwide, Farmer's program to teach adult illiterates how to read met with the president's wholehearted support.

Farmer subsequently set out to recruit other leaders to help him put his plan into effect. By mid-1965, Martin Luther King, Jr., John Lewis, and Whitney Young, as well as Vice-president Hubert H.

Presiding over a 1969 White House reception, President Richard Nixon shakes hands with Farmer, newly appointed assistant secretary in the Department of Health, Education, and Welfare. As one of the highest-ranking blacks in Nixon's Republican administration, Farmer did his best to advance civil rights; he felt he made little progress, however, and quit the job two years after taking it.

Humphrey and U.S. commissioner of education Howard Howe, were among those who had agreed to endorse Farmer's literacy program. All that remained was for it to be approved for federal funding by the Office of Economic Opportunity (OEO), an agency formed by the president to spearhead the War on Poverty.

When the OEO money came through, Farmer said privately, it would be a good time for him to leave CORE. He would resign from his post as national director to chair the Center for Community Action Education, the nonprofit organization he had set up in Washington, D.C., to coordinate the literacy program. He and his wife were so confident the OEO would approve the funding that they purchased a home in the nation's capital.

On Christmas Day, however, there arrived a most unwelcome present in the form of a front-page article in the *Washington Post*. The newspaper revealed Farmer's private plan to leave CORE, which thoroughly unsettled his co-workers. Moreover, the article spelled out the connection between the Center for Community Action Education and CORE and SNCC, two of the civil rights movement's most militant organizations. This disclosure sparked several congressmen and big-city mayors to prevail upon the Johnson administration to stop the OEO from funding Farmer's literacy program. Suddenly, what had seemed a sure thing appeared headed for certain defeat.

"We are being driven into a sea of illiteracy," lamented Farmer, who felt that the Johnson administration, in bowing to political pressure, had betrayed him. "They want the rain without the thunder and lightning, the ocean without the terrible roar. Nothing," he noted, "can be achieved without a struggle."

As his plans for a national literacy program unraveled, Farmer found himself without an organization to call his own. Now that it was widely known he had been planning to leave CORE, he could no longer head it effectively. In January 1966, Farmer agreed to resign as national director. His post was filled that March by Floyd McKissick, CORE's national chairman.

When Farmer ended his tenure with CORE, his career as a field-worker came to a close, too. For the next two years, he taught part-time at Lincoln University in Pennsylvania; in 1967, he also became an adjunct professor at New York University, where he offered a course on the civil rights movement. In his spare time, Farmer traveled the lecture circuit, speaking in support of both racial pride and interracial relations.

All told, these activities left Farmer feeling unsatisfied. He missed serving the public. Accordingly, when he was invited to run for a seat in the House of Representatives in a newly created congressional district in Brooklyn, he jumped at the chance. The time had finally come, he believed, for him to work on the inside toward achieving the goals he had long championed as an outsider.

Farmer was backed by the Liberal party, to which he had belonged for more than a decade, as well as by the Republican party. The Democrats had their own candidate: state assemblywoman Shirley Chisholm. Unfortunately for Farmer, the majority of the district's voters were registered Democrats, and on election day they voted along party lines. By soundly defeating Farmer, Chisholm became the nation's first black congresswoman.

Before long, another opportunity for Farmer to enter politics arose, this time from an unexpected quarter. Having publicly supported Hubert H. Humphrey, the Democratic candidate, in what turned out to be a losing bid for the presidency in the 1968 election, Farmer was surprised when newly elected president Richard M. Nixon offered him the post of

Martin Luther King, Jr., meets with veteran civil rights and union activist A. Philip Randolph at the 1965 Conference of Negro Leaders. Taking note of the victories recently won by the civil rights movement, Randolph— whom Farmer called "the grand old man"—observed that success might offer either "great opportunity" or "great danger" to the movement's future.

assistant secretary in the Department of Health, Education, and Welfare (HEW). Accepting the appointment would make Farmer the first black to become a high-ranking member of the Republican administration.

After careful deliberation, Farmer decided to accept the position. If the Nixon administration was looking for someone to serve as a liaison between the White House and black America, then that person had best be someone black Americans could count on. Farmer was sworn into office on April 2, 1969, and moved with his wife and two daughters to Washington, D.C.

From the outset, Farmer said of his new job, he attempted "to get on the inside and try to have some influence." Sadly, his efforts at HEW usually ended in disappointment. The administration's unwillingness to advance civil rights left him with the feeling that he was performing "a constant balancing act on the scales of my own conscience."

Finally, after serving as HEW's assistant secretary for nearly 2 years, the 50-year-old Farmer resigned from his government post. "The achievements are not sufficient or fast enough to satisfy my appetite for progress," he told reporters on December 8, 1970, the day after his resignation took effect. "I must confess that I chafe in the ponderous bureaucracy, and long, especially now, for my old role as advocate, critic, activist."

He did not get his wish, but he came close. After returning to the lecture circuit, Farmer linked forces with former CORE colleague Ruth Turner Perot and founded the Council on Minority Planning and Strategy (COMPAS), a think tank aimed at studying black issues. In the spring of 1973, COMPAS received enough federal funding to form the Public Policy Training Institute (PPTI). Over the next year, the PPTI conducted seminars on public policy for faculty members at predominantly black colleges in

the Washington, D.C., area. The seminars featured an impressive group of speakers, including U.S. senators Jacob Javits and Edward M. Kennedy, journalists Jack Anderson and Daniel Schorr, and consumer advocate Ralph Nader.

In 1975, Farmer helped to establish the Fund for an Open Society, a nonprofit company that provided low-interest mortgage loans "to persons of all colors who were making prointegration housing moves." That same year, he landed a job with the Coalition of American Public Employees (CAPE), an organization that lobbied for the rights of public workers. Eight months after joining CAPE, he became its executive director.

Just as Farmer settled into the new post, however, his life was thrown into turmoil. In 1976, Lula

Farmer, flanked by the Reverend Martin Luther King, Jr. (right), and King's aide, the Reverend Fred Shuttlesworth, prepares to join the historic 1965 march from Selma, Alabama, to Montgomery. Farmer revered King, but he urged restraint after the SCLC leader's 1968 assassination. "The only fitting memorial to this martyred leader," said Farmer, "is a monumental commitment—now, not a day later—to eliminate racism. Dr. King hated bloodshed. His own blood must not now trigger more bloodshed."

Teaching a class at Mary Washington College in Fredericksburg, Virginia, Farmer talks to students about the history—and the future—of the civil rights movement. The next century, he predicts, will be a "time not for jailgoing and bleeding heads, but for long-range planning and sophisticated strategizing." The future, he adds, "must see a rebuilding of black folk—a renaissance."

Farmer, his wife and companion for nearly 30 years, finally succumbed to Hodgkin's disease. James Farmer subsequently moved to Fredericksburg, Virginia, the same town in which the first Freedom Riders had initially come face-to-face with Jim Crow.

Farmer remained with CAPE until 1981. In his spare time, he strove to put his life in order by writing his autobiography, but he did not have an easy time of it. In 1979, a rare ailment caused his right eye to lose its power of sight. The disorder returned four years later, this time affecting his left eye; fortunately, advanced medical treatment managed to restore its vision partially. With the aid of a magnifying glass and a thick-tipped felt pen, he was able to complete *Lay Bare the Heart*, which was published in 1985.

By then, Farmer had become a professor at Mary Washington College in Fredericksburg. And he was still teaching the history of the civil rights movement as he entered his seventies half a decade later.

"I have helped to pave the roads on which America's black children walk toward new vistas," Farmer acknowledged in his autobiography. Yet he has been quick to say that "our nation deceives itself with the fiction that the task is complete and racism is dead and all is well." There are still places where Jim Crow lives, "where to be black is to be considered an enemy."

And so, according to James Farmer, there is still work to be done: "The tired among us must recharge our batteries. The uninitiated must learn to gird their loins. We have not finished the job of making our country whole." ❧

CHRONOLOGY

————— ❦ —————

1920   Born James Leonard Farmer, Jr., on January 12 in Marshall, Texas

1932   Wins a series of high school oratorical contests and is awarded a full college scholarship

1934   Graduates from high school; enrolls in Wiley College

1938   Graduates from Wiley; enrolls in the Howard University School of Religion

1941   Joins the Fellowship of Reconciliation (FOR); graduates from Howard University; becomes race relations secretary for the FOR in Chicago

1942   Organizes one of the nation's first sit-ins; cofounds the Committee [later Congress] of Racial Equality (CORE)

1943   Presides over the first national CORE conference

1945   Marries Winnie Christie; becomes a union organizer

1946   Divorces Christie

1949   Marries Lula Peterson; becomes student field secretary of the League for Industrial Democracy

1955   Resumes union organizing work

1959   First daughter, Tami Lynn, is born; Farmer becomes program director of the National Association for the Advancement of Colored People

1961   Becomes CORE's first national director; organizes the Freedom Rides; calls for a massive jail-in campaign in Mississippi; second daughter, Abbey Lee, is born

1962   Farmer begins CORE's Freedom Highways campaign

1963   Involves CORE in the March on Washington; becomes a founding member of the Council on United Civil Rights Leadership

1964   Announces CORE's New Directions program

1966   Resigns from CORE; becomes a professor at Pennsylvania's Lincoln University

1967   Becomes a professor at New York University

1968   Makes unsuccessful bid for Congress

1969   Becomes assistant secretary of the Department of Health, Education, and Welfare

1973   Founds the Public Policy Training Institute

1975   Establishes the Fund for an Open Society

1976   Becomes executive director of the Coalition of American Public Employees

1984   Becomes a professor at Mary Washington College

1985   Publishes autobiography, *Lay Bare the Heart*

1991   Continues to teach civil rights history at Mary Washington

FURTHER READING

—————

Barnes, Catherine A. *Journey from Jim Crow: The Desegregation of Southern Transit.* New York: Columbia University Press, 1983.

Bell, Inge Powell. *CORE and the Strategy of Nonviolence.* New York: Random House, 1968.

Farmer, James. *Freedom—When?* New York: Random House, 1965.

———. *Lay Bare the Heart: An Autobiography of the Civil Rights Movement.* New York: Arbor House, 1985.

Jakoubek, Robert. *Martin Luther King, Jr.* New York: Chelsea House, 1989.

Meier, August, and Elliott Rudwick. *CORE: A Study in the Civil Rights Movement, 1942–1968.* New York: Oxford University Press, 1973.

Morris, Aldon D. *The Origins of the Civil Rights Movement: Black Communities Organizing for Change.* New York: Free Press, 1984.

Peck, James. *Freedom Ride.* New York: Simon & Schuster, 1962.

Powledge, Fred. *Free at Last? The Civil Rights Movement and the People Who Made It.* Boston: Little, Brown, 1991.

Raines, Howell. *My Soul Is Rested: Movement Days in the Deep South Remembered.* New York: Putnam, 1977.

Rustin, Bayard. *Strategies for Freedom.* New York: Columbia University Press, 1976.

Weisbrot, Robert. *Freedom Bound: A History of America's Civil Rights Movement.* New York: Norton, 1990.

Williams, Juan. *Eyes on the Prize: America's Civil Rights Years, 1954–1965.* New York: Viking Penguin, 1987.

INDEX

PICTURE CREDITS

————— ✿ —————

JEFF SKLANSKY holds a bachelor's degree in history from the University of California, Berkeley, and a master's degree in American history from Columbia University, where he is currently earning a Ph.D. He is a former newspaper reporter.

NATHAN IRVIN HUGGINS is W.E.B. Du Bois Professor of History and Director of the W.E.B. Du Bois Institute for Afro-American Research at Harvard University. He previously taught at Columbia University. Professor Huggins is the author of numerous books, including *Black Odyssey: The Afro-American Ordeal in Slavery*, *The Harlem Renaissance*, and *Slave and Citizen: The Life of Frederick Douglass*.